THE
DELETED E-MAILS OF
HILLARY CLINTON

Also by John Moe

★

Dear Luke, We Need to Talk, Darth: And Other
Pop Culture Correspondences

THE
DELETED E-MAILS OF
HILLARY CLINTON

★ ★ ★ *A Parody* ★ ★ ★

As obtained by WikiLoox and smuggled to
JOHN MOE

THREE RIVERS PRESS • NEW YORK

Published in the United States by Three Rivers Press, an imprint of the Crown
Publishing Group, a division of Penguin Random House LLC, New York.
www.crownpublishing.com

Three Rivers Press and the Tugboat design are registered trademarks of
Penguin Random House LLC.

E-mail backgrounds: Picsfive/Shutterstock
Page 11: RetroClipArt/Veer
Pages 16, 75, 95, 105: Cindy Luu
Page 25, top: Paul Matthew Photography/Shutterstock
Page 25, bottom: Stokkete/Shutterstock
Page 26, top: Blend Images Photography/Veer
Page 26, bottom: Gerville/iStock
Page 27, top: Blend Images Photography/Veer
Page 27, bottom: Sheftsoff Women Girls/Shutterstock
Page 28: Alloy Photography/Veer

Library of Congress Cataloging-in-Publication Data

Moe, John, 1968–
The deleted e-mails of Hillary Clinton: a parody / John Moe. —First edition.
        pages   cm
1. Clinton, Hillary Rodham—Miscellanea. 2. Clinton, Hillary Rodham—
Humor. 3. Electronic mail messages—Humor. 4. United States—Politics and
government—2009—Humor. 5. Women presidential candidates—United States—
Humor. 6. Presidents' spouses—United States—Humor. I. Title.
E887.C55M64 2015
327.730092—dc23   2015026687

ISBN 978-1-101-90607-1
eBook ISBN 978-1-101-90608-8

PRINTED IN THE UNITED STATES OF AMERICA

Book design by Elizabeth Rendfleisch
Illustrations by Cindy Luu
Cover design by Tal Goretsky

1 3 5 7 9 10 8 6 4 2

First Edition

CONTENTS

ATTENTION!

You are about to read documents that the United States government does not want you to read. Enclosed in this dossier are e-mails to and from Hillary Clinton during her tenure as Secretary of State, sent and received through an account that ordinary people were never supposed to find out about.

These are the e-mails supposedly deleted from her own private server, before they could ever be turned over to any authorities.

This is the personal stuff. The shocking stuff.

Why are we showing this to you? Who are we, anyway?

We are WikiLoox. We are a group of ingenious cyber freedom fighters who comb the remote recesses of the deep Web to gain access to secret governmental documents. Then we release those documents to the world. We believe that there should be no secrets in the world. As for our membership, we don't want to give anyone our names because we don't want to get into trouble.

We are not Democrats. We are not Republicans. We think the whole system is rotten and corrupt. We don't read corporate newspapers. We don't watch the news on TV. We don't keep up on things. We don't know what's going on. But we believe in one thing: freedom.

How we got these e-mails is not important. Maybe we were tipped off by some important Washington insider. Maybe we saw an interview with Hillary Clinton and she had the login and password written on a note on her desk. Maybe Hillary Clinton is one of us. She's not, of course, but wouldn't that be amazing? But again, she is not part of our group.

So read on, my friend. Read on for freedom.

Love,
WikiLoox

★ ★ ★ ★ ★ ★ ★ ★ ★

2009

★ ★ ★ ★ ★ ★ ★ ★ ★

TO: Barack Obama
FROM: HRC
Subject: It being fine

Barack,

Tomorrow we begin a new journey together. You, as President of the United States, and me, as Secretary of State, which is a different job entirely. I just want you to know that I am honored to serve under you and have you as my boss.

It's fine.

Certainly, we fought hard against each other through a protracted primary process, one that became rather bitter and testy at times, but that is all in the past. Now I'm ready to serve in this other job while you serve as President and live in the White House.

I will live somewhere else. And that is fine with me. I can live a lot of other places. That's no big deal.

It's fine.

I am eager to get started in my new role and excited to do my part to help establish peace and harmony between the United States and other nations, just as I've been eager to establish peace and harmony between you, the President, and me, just the Secretary of State.

I'm totally okay.

HRC

P.S. I may use this e-mail account from time to time. That's fine, right?

January 20, 2009

TO: HRC
FROM: Barack Obama
RE: It being fine

Madam Secretary,

Thank you for your note of encouragement. I'm perfectly fine with you using a personal e-mail account. I mean, who cares, right? I don't think anyone would really get upset about it even if they found out.

Besides, this way we can exchange information about the secret inner workings of power. I'm talking about stuff like Area 51, who killed JFK, and our secret plan to personally break into people's homes and steal their guns. Kidding! We'll hire people to break into the homes. Kidding again! Seriously, though, I'm excited to find out about UFOs. And Bigfoots. Bigfeet?

Actually, come to think of it, I'm not sure you get to know all those things. Maybe it's just a President thing. Bill probably knew about it when he was President. And I'll find out because I'll be President. But you might not find out ever at all. Since you're not President.

Again, really looking forward to what we can do together!

Barack

January 22, 2009

TO: Campaign advisors
FROM: HRC
Subject: Just for laughs

Hi all,

Been thinking we really need to get the whole team together
for drinks and catch up on what we've all been up to since the
campaign. Obviously, given my profile, it couldn't be at Chili's or
anything, but there is a secure bunker beneath my office. We could
sit around the table there. And drink. And talk. Fun, right?!

Also, I had a really crazy idea. Wouldn't it be a riot if we did some
polling to see what would happen if I ran against Obama in '12?
Just to be silly! And to find out! Totally random idea, I promise you.

You must tell absolutely no one that I'm very seriously considering
this completely crazy nutty notion! Ha ha! Because I'm not. Yes. I
am, though. Not. Do it.

HRC

January 23, 2009

TO: Campaign advisors
FROM: HRC
RE: Just for laughs

Well, I didn't get replies from any of you on this. I guess everyone's
super busy! Me too! Please delete this thread.

HRC

TO: Huma Abedin
FROM: HRC
Subject: Urgent

Huma, we have a big adventure ahead of us. You're my right-hand woman, my confidante, my assistant, my friend. You are the "Golden Girls" wrapped into one.

Here's the thing.

I'm going to be traveling a lot for this job. All over the world. Important high-level meetings with world leaders. Peace in the Middle East? Might be up to me to pull that one off. Repairing America's image with the global community? On my shoulders. These shoulders. Right here. You can't see me but I'm pointing to my shoulders.

To get this done the right way, I'm going to need one thing above everything else: Pantsuits. That's what I'm going to wear. A whole lot of pantsuits.

To date, my pantsuit game has been, at times, acceptable, but ultimately insufficient. My designated pantsuit vendor has been good enough for the Senate, but I am no longer one of a hundred. I am THE Secretary of State. Could I have won the presidential nomination with better pantsuitsmanship? Who's to say? But it might have made the difference. Now that I'm on a world stage, I need to go up a level.

I want you to get me the top pantsuit wrangler in the world today and hire him or her. I'm not talking about someone who's good with all sorts of clothes. No. I want a specialist. As Michael Phelps is to swimming, this person needs to be to pantsuits.

We can pay this person whatever we can, and if that's not enough, I've got a bunch of money saved up from giving speeches to augment the salary.

I'm using this e-mail just in case we ever get subpoenaed. I don't want someone to think I'm obsessed with pantsuits. It's just that I want the best pantsuits and the best pantsuit wrangler on the planet and I'm obsessed by it. Understood?

HRC

January 24, 2009

TO: HRC
FROM: Huma Abedin
RE: Urgent

Yes, ma'am. You want someone who's very good at pantsuits. On it.

January 24, 2009

TO: Huma Abedin
FROM: HRC
RE: Urgent

NO! I don't want "very good." Foghat was very good. I want the Beatles, the Stones, and Nirvana. Of pantsuits.

HRC

★ ★ ★

January 26, 2009

TO: HRC
FROM: Mr. Pantsuit
Subject: How are you doing?

Hello Madam Secretary!

Congratulations on your new position! It is richly deserved! All of us here at Mr. Pantsuit are so proud of you. And we are proud to be your provider of pantsuits ever since your first campaign for the Senate in 2000. Every time we see you on television, giving important speeches and the like, we are all so excited that it's a Mr. Pantsuit pantsuit that you are wearing.

It's true that we are not a large business, just a small handful of employees who believe in our customers and BELIEVE IN PANTSUITS. Truth be told, you are pretty much our only customer.

And that is what has made the last few months so difficult, ever since you got the new job. Each day begins with all the employees asking each other, "Did she call today?" only to learn that no, you did not.

Are you okay?

You are everything to us. You are the sun and the moon. No one has done for pantsuits what you have done for pantsuits. Have we failed you?

Love,
The Staff of Mr. Pantsuit

January 27, 2009

TO: Mr. Pantsuit
FROM: HRC
RE: How are you doing?

Please contact my office for an update on this matter.

HRC

★ ★ ★

February 3, 2009

TO: HRC
FROM: Bill
Subject: Are we having fun yet?!

Hey there!

Hope you're settling in okay. Remember: it's a perfectly good place to work, do good for the world, and make up your mind about what you might want to do in 2016. Or 2012? Forget I said that.

Anyhoo, things are great in New York. Jimmy Fallon and I had a rollerblade race through Central Park and then went to see Jersey Boys. Awesome. I've seen it before but it's still just as good.

So good luck with solving the whole Israel-Palestine thing.

B

★ ★ ★

February 15, 2009

TO: Huma Abedin
FROM: HRC
Subject: Dates down the road

I want to check possible availability for a few potential guests either on Inauguration Day of 2012 or Inauguration Day of 2016. Especially 2012. I can't tell you what the event is.

Please see if the following have those dates free or can make them available:

Joni Mitchell
Fleetwood Mac
Bob Dylan
The Rolling Stones

No reason. There's no hidden agenda behind this inquiry. Just want to know. That's all. No big deal. And this is completely top secret. But I'm just wondering.

HRC

February 15, 2009

TO: HRC
FROM: Huma Abedin
RE: Dates down the road

Happy to look into it. My hunch is that it might be a bit early for some of these groups to know their schedules so far in advance.

BTW, if you're going for big names, I could check in with Prince. His music is great, he can be pretty weird, but he might be just weird enough to book himself this far out.

Huma

February 15, 2009

TO: Huma Abedin
FROM: HRC
RE: Dates down the road

Prince? Ha! Confession time: I used to have a TOTAL crush on Prince. But I'm over that now. I really am.

★ ★ ★

February 23, 2009

TO: Secretary Clinton, Secretary Gates, Secretary Salazar, Secretary Locke, Secretary Shinseki, Secretary Chu, Secretary Napolitano, Secretary Geithner, Secretary Solis, Secretary Vilsack, Secretary Sebelius, Secretary LaHood, Secretary Donovan
FROM: Barack Obama
Subject: Important work to be done

Hello everyone,

I just want to say how delighted I am that you are a part of my administration. Together, we will make America a better place and help the hard-working people of this great nation to improve their lives. It's important work.

With that in mind, I have a very important message for all you secretaries:

This coffee isn't going to fetch itself!

Okay, you crazy kooks. Catch you later.

Barack

February 23, 2009

TO: Barack Obama
FROM: HRC
RE: Important work to be done

Dear Mr. President,

Your attempt at humor is actually quite insulting, especially to Secretary Sebelius, Secretary Solis, Secretary Napolitano, and me. We are women of great professional accomplishment, entrusted by you and confirmed by Congress to lead major departments in the U.S. government.

Your attempt at humor, however, is mired in a Mad Men-era psychology of women being subservient to their male bosses. You should know that the modern administrative assistant or executive assistant no longer fetches coffee for anyone.

So I would appreciate no further mockery of gendered stereotypes or our positions as members of this administration.

Hillary Clinton
Secretary of State

February 23, 2009

TO: HRC
FROM: Barack Obama
RE: Important work to be done

Madam Secretary,

I sincerely apologize for my earlier e-mail. Though it was written in jest, it was insensitive and unfair as well as degrading to women. I am in the process of calling all the esteemed members of the cabinet on that e-mail to verbally express my regret and remorse for sending such a message.

It won't happen again.

Barack

February 23, 2009

TO: Barack Obama
FROM: HRC
RE: Important work to be done

I GOT YOU! HAHAHAHAHAHAHA! I burned you so bad! You totally bought it that I was all mad at you! SUCKAAAAAA!

HRC

February 23, 2009

TO: HRC
FROM: Barack Obama
RE: Important work to be done

Oh my God. You did. You totally got me. Hook, line, and sinker.

I'm gonna get you back, Hillary, just you wait.

February 23, 2009

TO: Barack Obama
FROM: HRC
RE: Important work to be done

Plenty of time for that after I defeat you four years from now.

February 23, 2009

TO: HRC
FROM: Barack Obama
RE: Important work to be done

What?

February 23, 2009

TO: Barack Obama
FROM: HRC
RE: Important work to be done

Kidding again! Ha ha!

Never mind.

H

★ ★ ★

March 8, 2009

TO: HRC
FROM: Huma Abedin
Subject: Update

Madam Secretary,

I have very exciting news about our pantsuit situation. Lance of Cleveland has agreed to come aboard as our new Senior Pantsuit Consultant, pending your approval, of course. I'm sure I don't need to tell you about Lance of Cleveland's stellar reputation and his preeminence as the most famous and critically acclaimed pantsuit designer in the business. He is the biggest name in all of Cleveland, which, as we all know, is the pantsuit capital of the world.

Lance has already sent over some sketches he would like to see you wear on upcoming trips. As I'm hoping you'll agree, these pantsuits are practical, discrete, sincere, in short, they are magnificent.

"Peacock of Freedom"

"Liberty Is on the Catwalk"

"The Star-Spangled Stunner"

If you like them, the only thing left to set is his pay rate.

THE DELETED E-MAILS OF HILLARY CLINTON

March 8, 2009

TO: Huma Abedin
FROM: HRC
RE: Update

Pay it. Pay him what he wants.

This is excellent.

With the right pantsuits, a person can achieve anything. That is not just what I believe, it is needlepointed on a sampler I keep atop my dresser. As to whether I also have this as a tattoo, I cannot discuss that.

Thank you.

HRC

★   ★   ★

March 31, 2009

TO: The Fun Four
FROM: HRC
Subject: New e-mail address

Hi Ladies!

Just wanted to let everyone know to use this address only going forward. Nothing against my official government e-mail or my several dozen other private e-mail addresses set up as decoys, but this is the one we should use to really chat among the four of us.

That way, no one will suspect our plot to seize global power and rule as a four-headed tyrant. Ha ha! Just kidding. That is a total overstatement.

Wouldn't it be fun, though? Hillary, Gwyneth, Beyoncé, Oprah? They could call us Hilwynbeyprah. Kind of catchy.

Anyways, the real reason I'm writing is to say we need to have another girls' weekend! Beyoncé, you did such a great job hosting in the secret underground caverns beneath your Hamptons estate last time. And Gwynnie, the yurt castle in Nepal you used the time before was top-notch. I would volunteer to host but I am just so busy with the new job and everything, along with trying to solve my pantsuit crisis. Opes, you up for hosting?

H

March 31, 2009

TO: The Fun Four
FROM: Oprah
RE: New e-mail address

First, totally agree about world domination. Not something we should be daydreaming about constantly at this point in time. Would be a total headache. For the moment.

I was actually thinking Opwynbeylary instead of Hilwynbeyprah. Catchier.

Second, sure I'm up for hosting! Chicago is a total pain for traffic so I was thinking maybe my ice fortress in Greenland? It's still completely isolated and does not appear on charts. And it has a runway now.

Oprah

March 31, 2009

TO: The Fun Four
FROM: Gwyneth
RE: New e-mail address

Sounds fun! And great news about the runway. I remember last time having to skydive in there while loaded down with a variety of body creams, salves, and all-natural accoutrements. Made landing difficult, especially on ice. I sprained my ankle but was fortunately able to heal it based on some advice I had given myself.

Agree: Overthrowing governments as Opwynbeylary is unworkable. For now.

Gwynnie

March 31, 2009

TO: The Fun Four
FROM: Beyoncé
RE: New e-mail address

MY DEAR FRIENDS,

OPWYNBEYLARY.
OPWYNBEYLARY.
OPWYNBEYLARY.

ALL SHALL BE ONE. ONE SHALL BE ALL. THE ROOSTER WILL CROW. THE CROW WILL ROOST.

OPWYNBEYLARY.

BEY

March 31, 2009

TO: The Fun Four
FROM: HRC
RE: New e-mail address

Beyoncé,

You okay? You're coming off a little . . . intense?

H

March 31, 2009

TO: The Fun Four
FROM: Beyoncé
RE: New e-mail address

ALL IS WELL. INTENSITY IS NECESSARY IN ORDER TO ACCOMPLISH MY GOALS.

BEY

TO: Huma Abedin
FROM: HRC
Subject: Pets?

I've been thinking about my public image. I know I come off kind of cold to people, standoffish, more of a policy wonk than a human being. Maybe getting a pet of some kind would help with that? Articles in People with the new pet, showing off my softer side? I know Bill has had his dog, but I'm thinking something particular to me.

Ideas:

- Ocelot. Lots of people have cats, but maybe I get a larger, more powerful cat that people wouldn't mess with. Or a lynx?

- Goldfish. Low maintenance. Always easy to find, reliable. Those are good qualities.

- Salmon. Same but larger.

- Shark. Definitely strong. Higher maintenance, though.

- Ant farm. Inspiring work ethic. Hard to take out for walks.

- Guinea pig. Cute, simple. But pretty much a hairy rock that screams.

- Wolf. Beautiful animal, could intimidate other world leaders. Perhaps a bit too terrifying?

- Ferret. Might need votes from the Renaissance Faire crowd at some point. Still, seems like kind of a high price to pay for those votes.

- Bees. I wonder if I could have some hives installed around the office. They're industrious, which is good, and could lead to a cutdown of unnecessary meetings.

I'll keep thinking.

HRC

★ ★ ★

May 12, 2009

TO: HRC
FROM: Bill
Subject: Water-skiing

Oh hey. Long time no talk and all that.

Listen, I thought it would be fun for you and me to grab a few friends, rent a boat, fill up a cooler with Bud Lights, and hit the lake for some water-skiing. Just cut loose, you know? Make a weekend of it.

Or Jet Skis. We could do Jet Skis. Go out, get drunk, get stupid, have fun. You in?

Bill

May 12, 2009

TO: Bill
FROM: HRC
RE: Water-skiing

I have to work.

I am the Secretary of State.

Other reasons I couldn't do this: I don't "get drunk" or "get stupid," I don't water-ski, I am not in a position where I can be seen cutting loose, there are no friends I can think of whom I would want to spend a weekend with, Jet Skis are horrible for the environment, and the whole trip just sounds awful.

Hillary

May 12, 2009

TO: HRC
FROM: Bill
RE: Water-skiing

Honey, I know. I was just joking around.

It's cool with you if I go, though, right?

DiCaprio is gonna be there. Some of the guys from Bon Jovi. Andre Agassi, maybe. It's gonna be awesome. Joe Walsh might stop by.

Proud of you,
Bill

June 10, 2009

TO: Mitch McConnell, Grover Norquist, Paul Ryan, Nancy Pelosi, John McCain, Antonin Scalia, Chris Matthews
FROM: HRC
Subject: Hand-Painted Figurine Club

We are all Washington insiders. We are often at one another's throats about issues of policy and government. Our careers, in many cases, are built on the division between red states and blue states in America.

But some of you have been slipping. I've heard complex legislation described as "needing a very fine brush" and "adorably intricate." People are going to ask questions. We cannot let that happen.

So let's review.

RULES OF HAND-PAINTED FIGURINE CLUB

1. Do not talk about Hand-Painted Figurine Club.

2. DO NOT TALK ABOUT HAND-PAINTED FIGURINE CLUB.

3. Everyone uses top security measures to not be spotted attending Hand-Painted Figurine Club.

4. Everyone brings their own brushes and leaves with their own brushes.

5. Humans (babies, small children) and animals are acceptable figurines.

6. Dungeons & Dragons figures are tolerated but not encouraged, Scalia.

7. DO NOT TALK ABOUT HAND-PAINTED FIGURINE CLUB.

Next meeting will be at McConnell's place at the regular time. Future meetings will be announced verbally so that there is no written or electronic trail. Delete this e-mail.

HRC

TO: HRC
FROM: Michelle Obama
Subject: How do you even deal?

Hillary,

You've been in this business for a lot longer than Barack and me. And a lot of people dislike you. A lot. How do you deal with all the hate out there? Makes me all

June 16, 2009

TO: Michelle Obama
FROM: HRC
RE: How do you even deal?

It's not easy, Michelle. But you can't read stuff online. It drives me

TO: HRC
FROM: Michelle Obama
RE: How do you even deal?

I know I shouldn't, but I'm all like

June 16, 2009

TO: Michelle Obama
FROM: HRC
RE: How do you even deal?

Try this—just close your eyes and imagine what you'd do if you could get someone like Maureen Dowd, but definitely not Maureen Dowd, in a room. Kind of like

June 16, 2009

TO: HRC
FROM: Michelle Obama
RE: How do you even deal?

Like this?

June 16, 2009

TO: Michelle Obama
FROM: HRC
RE: How do you even deal?

TO: HRC
FROM: Michelle Obama
RE: How do you even deal?

★ ★ ★

TO: Lance of Cleveland
FROM: HRC
Subject: Thank you

Lance of Cleveland,

May I just say again what an honor it is to have you on the team. Your pantsuitsmanship is unparalleled and will certainly help America and me as well. To date, I have loved the pantsuits you have made me, especially the more subtle and conservative ones.

I have some concerns about your pantsuit mockups for my trip to Africa.

Lion King pantsuit—I loved the movie, everyone did, but having EVERY character depicted on a pantsuit seems a bit distracting. Also, not sure what message that sends.

Preferred country pantsuit—A diplomat's role is to be presentable and approachable by the entire global community. Highlighting the flags of only SOME countries would be problematic. Not sure how the hearts around the Israeli flag will play, for instance.

1,000 Hillary faces pantsuit—I know I'm trying to make an impression, but a thousand pictures of me on one pantsuit seems a bit much.

I love the ingenuity and the creativity. I think for this trip, let's stick with gray and dark green.

HRC

TO: HRC
FROM: Bill
Subject: Kinshasa

So let me get this straight: you're in the city of Kinshasa, you're on a tour of Africa because you are the SECRETARY OF STATE, and someone asks you what MISTER Clinton thinks about a Chinese trade deal with the Democratic Republic of Congo? Hoo man, I do NOT know how you held it together.

B

August 11, 2009

TO: Bill
FROM: HRC
RE: Kinshasa

Not sure I really did hold it together. I think I said something like "Wait, you want me to tell you what my husband thinks? My husband is not the Secretary of State, I am. So you ask my opinion, I will tell you my opinion. I am not going to be channeling my husband."

Not the greatest day.

H

August 11, 2009

TO: HRC
FROM: Bill
RE: Kinshasa

Sorry to hear about it, even though it was pretty dang funny. It's been pretty tough up here at James Taylor's place on Martha's Vineyard too. Just last night, JT broke a string on his guitar AND we almost ran out of lobster.

Then Goldie Hawn INSISTED that we go to the go-kart rental place, but they were closed so we borrowed (stole?) some dune buggies and were out all night. It was hilarious.

Hey, just checking on this because I don't know for sure: you want me to fly out there and give a hand? Let people know what I think, get interviewed on TV, glad-hand a few reporters? Would that help?

B

August 11, 2009

TO: Bill
FROM: HRC
RE: Kinshasa

NO!

August 11, 2009

TO: HRC
FROM: Bill
RE: Kinshasa

Gotcha. Okay. Gotta run. John Stamos just showed up with a Frisbee.

B

September 12, 2009

TO: HRC
FROM: Toni Morrison
Subject: Me

Hillary. I heard about your cabal. I don't know what you're up to but I bet it's big. You, Oprah, Gwyneth Paltrow, some pop singer. I want in. For crying out loud, one can only be a wise and lyrical novelist for so long before one craves POWER. I think you have it. I KNOW you'll have more. I want in. I crave true power. It has eluded me so often.

Let me in, Hillary. Sign me up. Now. Please.

TM

September 12, 2009

TO: Toni Morrison
FROM: HRC
RE: Me

Toni! So great to hear from you. Frankly, I don't know which surprises me more: the complete absence of complex analogies and historical references in your e-mail or the fact that you seem to be on to us. Winking emoticon. I don't know how emoticons work so just imagine a winking one there.

I'll need to check with the gals and get back to you.

★ ★ ★

TO: The Fun Four
FROM: HRC
Subject: Fun Five?

Ladies,

Toni Morrison wants in. I know the knee-jerk response is to say no because what we have among the four of us is extremely potent and valuable. We have Oscars (Gwyneth), Grammys (Beyoncé), Massive Governmental Influence (Yours Truly), and Oprah (Oprah). But Toni has National Book Awards and a Pulitzer, and would give us a foothold in literature, an area we don't have as yet.

I'm cautious, yes, but our rules state that we have to be unanimous.

Opwynbeylary. OpwynbeylaryNI?

H

September 13, 2009

TO: The Fun Four
FROM: Oprah
RE: Fun Five?

Toni is a dear friend and an inspiration. I do question whether she'd be able to safely perform any skydiving that might come up, but on the other hand I know she's strong. I saw Toni Morrison kill a bear with her fists once.

Yeah, I'm in.

O

TO: The Fun Four
FROM: Gwyneth
RE: Fun Five?

I will vote yes, as well. The inspiration she brought to me as an artist, a lifestyle guru, a celebrity, I really am not sure what I am, you guys. Anyway, I like her books.

Gwyneth

September 13, 2009

TO: The Fun Four
FROM: Beyoncé
RE: Fun Five?

SHE SHALL NOT BE AMONG US. I FORBID IT. THERE CAN BE ONLY FOUR. THUS SPAKE THE PROPHECY AND THUS THE PROPHECY WILL BE FULFILLED.

I CONTROL DRAGONS AND I SHALL PREVENT TONI MORRISON FROM ENTERING OUR CABAL/FUN CIRCLE.

I LITERALLY CONTROL DRAGONS. THIS IS NOT METAPHOR.

SINCERELY,
BEY

★ ★ ★

October 1, 2009

TO: Huma Abedin
FROM: HRC
Subject: Berlin trip

As you all know, I will be traveling to Germany to commemorate the 20th anniversary of the fall of the Berlin Wall. I was remembering the tremendous energy and spirit that accompanied that event all those years ago and it got me thinking: what if we celebrated the fall of this terrible barrier with a rock concert?

Off the top of my head, I thought perhaps Prince would be a good choice. He has an international following and everyone loves him. He could ride with me on the plane. That would be fine.

Just a thought. But let's do it, okay?

HRC

October 3, 2009

TO: HRC
FROM: Scheduling Office
Subject: FW: Berlin trip

Hi Hillary,

Our scheduling office has investigated your idea and found that, just as we suspected, Prince would be unavailable for this event. He's at his Paisley Park studio that whole time; apparently he's scheduled to watch Finding Nemo thirty times in a row at that time. No one is sure why. Further, the commemoration is slated to be a more formal affair so a rock concert would be out of place.

Sorry to disappoint you.

October 4, 2009

TO: Huma Abedin
FROM: HRC
RE: Berlin trip

Huma,

I wonder if he'd feel different if I invited him personally. Can you get me his phone number? His home phone number, I mean.

Besides, I want to talk to him about some official State Department business. And all of this is secret and no one can know about this. But it's all okay.

HRC

October 4, 2009

TO: HRC
FROM: Huma Abedin
RE: Berlin trip

Okay. I will try.

And, just to be sure, this correspondence is happening *exclusively* on your private e-mail, right? So what we're doing here is not part of the official public record?

Huma

October 4, 2009

TO: Huma Abedin
FROM: HRC
RE: Berlin trip

The number, Huma. That's all you need to do.

HRC

October 7, 2009

TO: HRC
FROM: Lance of Cleveland
Subject: Ideas for Berlin

Madam,

The collapse of the Berlin Wall was one of the most dramatic events of the 20th century. For your trip to commemorate it, I was thinking a gray pantsuit that appears, at first, to be quite ordinary.

But as the event moves along, bits of the gray fabric start to fall away—like a concrete wall!—revealing stones and powder underneath! Rebar begins to be exposed (it's actually pipe cleaner!) and tiny fabric people appear on your shoulders! The people are hoisted up there by a series of fishing line pulleys I operate underneath the stage.

All the world will see you and say "THERE is a leader. THERE is a diplomat. THERE IS A PANTSUIT."

Or brown. We could just go with brown.

I'll get to work on brown.

Lance of Cleveland

November 28, 2009

TO: HRC
FROM: Chelsea
Subject: So much to be done!

Mom!

It's so hard to believe that Marc and I are getting married *this* summer! We're in the process of interviewing wedding planner candidates right now, and I'll be sure that we keep whomever we pick in close contact with your office so everything can go smoothly.

I want you to know that we are eager for your participation in the planning process but that we recognize that your schedule is, of course, very busy. Still, if you have any thoughts on music, flowers, entertainment, or whatever, just let me know.

Also wanted to ask you about something. I LOVED it when Dad was President and you guys made the reporters stay away from me. It really helped to have as normal a childhood as I could have hoped to have. Thank you. I'm wondering, though, if that ban could be lifted now. Often I'll be at a social event with Marc and word will get out that I'm there. At that point, anyone remotely involved with journalism will sprint for the exits. It's very awkward, especially at dinner parties. I am 29 years old.

What have you told these people?

Love you!

C

November 28, 2009

TO: Chelsea
FROM: HRC
RE: So much to be done!

Honey,

All those reporters are totally overreacting. All I did was politely ask them to give you some personal space. Then I asked about their houses, for which I knew all the addresses. Then I complimented them by saying that they had lovely homes and it would be a shame if those homes were burned to the ground late one night. Which is true! It would be a shame.

As for the wedding, I'm sure you'll pick a marvelous planner who will perfectly capture what you and Marc have always dreamed of. I love you both so much. But let me put out one word for you: Prince.

For the reception? Right? How great would that be? Just putting it out there.

Mom

TO: HRC
FROM: Barack Obama
Subject: Subtlety

Hi Hillary,

Couple of things. First, as we near the end of 2009, I really want to congratulate you on a very successful first year as Secretary of State. You have done great work on trips to Asia, Africa, and Europe. You've provided a wise and informed presence as the United States' representative in areas like climate change and trade, and you've fostered improved relations with countries around the globe.

Second, you'll recall that during our meeting the other day in the Oval Office, I had to step out for a couple of minutes. When I returned, I noticed that you were literally measuring the drapes. Frankly, it's a bit difficult to get around the symbolism of that act. I'm just going to come right out and ask: are you planning to make a run for the presidency yourself? Will this happen in 2016 or—and this would change things quite a bit—earlier?

I'm writing on your private e-mail address so this is just between us.

Barack

December 10, 2009

TO: Barack Obama
FROM: HRC
RE: Subtlety

Barack, nothing could be further from my mind. I am 100% focused on performing my extensive duties as Secretary of State.

THE DELETED E-MAILS OF HILLARY CLINTON

Was I measuring drapes in the Oval Office? Yes. Had I brought my own tape measure? Yes, I had. But this was just because I had noticed the drapes in a previous meeting and thought that they had become shorter since Bill was in office.

It was all about drapes. I'm just very interested in drapes. That's all.

HRC

December 10, 2009

TO: HRC
FROM: Barack Obama
RE: Subtlety

And the book of fabric swatches in your briefcase?

December 10, 2009

TO: Barack Obama
FROM: HRC
RE: Subtlety

Oh, those? Ha! That's the White House book of fabric swatches, originally started by Mary Todd Lincoln. I had gotten it from Barbara Bush and handed it down to Laura Bush. I only had it that day because Laura wanted me to give it to Michelle. Did I forget? Whoops! Ha. I'll bring it over soon. The book of fabric swatches.

December 10, 2009

TO: HRC, Barack Obama
FROM: Joe Biden
RE: Subtlety

I love drapes too!

December 10, 2009

TO: Joe Biden, HRC
FROM: Barack Obama
RE: Subtlety

Dammit, Joe! How did you even get this e-mail?!

December 18, 2009

TO: HRC
FROM: HRC
Subject: Note to Self: Eleanor Roosevelt

Need trusted advisor. Ideal candidate? Eleanor Roosevelt.

PRO: My biggest inspiration, top role model ever.
CON: Currently dead.

Install portal to heaven at Department of State?

PRO: Convenient, would give Eleanor an easy commute.
CON: Physically, mathematically, and spiritually impossible.

Hold séances when I need to consult Eleanor on really tough issues?

PRO: She might be more amenable to working with/for me if not required to keep regular office hours, candle smell could make workplace pleasant for all.
CON: All that tedious chanting, fear of germs from holding hands with psychic.

Hire historical reenactor to portray Eleanor?

PRO: An actor gets a job, maybe persuade Meryl to take the gig?
CON: I would know it wasn't the real Eleanor.

Table the idea for now, get back to it later.

★ ★ ★ ★ ★ ★ ★ ★ ★ ★

2010

★ ★ ★ ★ ★ ★ ★ ★ ★ ★

TO: Campaign Advisors
FROM: HRC
Subject: The Future

Team,

I just want to make something very, very clear. I will NOT be running for President in 2012. I will not be challenging my dear friend Barack Obama for the Democratic nomination. I will not be running as the representative of the Hillary! Party, even though, anecdotally, I am told I could do quite well. I won't be running as a Republican, despite these repeated rumors that I am being courted by the GOP. I really don't know how these rumors get started because they are crazy. I guess it's because the Republican field looks about as strong as Emily Dickinson at a powerlifting contest but, again, it's not for me to say.

No, all these rumors and speculation must stop. I am dedicated to my very challenging position at the State Department. And I support the leadership provided by President Obama.

I hope this puts this matter to rest.

HRC

January 12, 2010

TO: HRC
FROM: John Boehner
RE: The Future

Hillary,

Look, I tried. And you said no. And that's fine. But when I met you in the alley behind Olive Garden in Alexandria, Virginia, to talk about you running as a Republican, I made it clear that this needed to be a secret offer. We got a guy running whose experience was that he ran a chain of pizza restaurants. We're not doing well. I can't let it get out that I pursued you, our greatest enemy, someone who stands for all we stand against, as a potential candidate.

So when I read this e-mail, I was dismayed. We both know that the quickest way to get rumors to spread is to look like you're trying to stop those rumors from spreading.

Boehner

January 12, 2010

TO: John Boehner
FROM: HRC
RE: The Future

I do apologize for that, John. Best of luck to you, Newt Gingrich, the pizza guy, assorted Mormons and fundamentalists, and whatever third-tier Bush family member you're able to pry loose from an oil field.

And as for the 2016 presidential election, I think we can agree that it is far too early to start thinking about those possibilities over and over and over.

HRC

January 12, 2010

TO: HRC
FROM: John Boehner
RE: The Future

What? I didn't even mention 2016.

★　★　★

TO: The Fun Four
FROM: HRC
Subject: Fun question

Ladies,

I was on one of my interminable international flights recently, and I had read all my prep materials and watched every movie on the plane. I watched Purple Rain, Under the Cherry Moon, Graffiti Bridge, everything. One of my staffers lent me some DVDs of a program called Sex and the City. Have you seen it? It's pretty fun and it's about four friends! Like us! Except they don't have to be secretive and they're not very ambitious.

It made me think about which of the characters we each are in our own group. I think I'm the Carrie of the group. I have an ongoing, sometimes challenging relationship with the central man in my life. And just as Carrie wrote a lot about New York, I had a lot written ABOUT me when I was the Senator from New York.

Which character do you think you are?

Hills

TO: The Fun Four
FROM: Gwyneth
RE: Fun question

I was actually up for a part on that show but I didn't get hired because they said I was too "esoteric" and didn't look like I had ever "eaten food." So I've always resented it and haven't watched it.

I had Lunchtime Nanny stay late yesterday and offer me her opinion on this subject. She says that I am most like Charlotte. I assume that Charlotte is just an average mom with an average number of millions of dollars who lives in a series of average homes and is married to an average rock superstar and who makes an average number of superhero movies.

Gwynnie

TO: The Fun Four
FROM: Oprah
RE: Fun question

What kind of bubble are you ladies living in that you haven't seen SATC? I had time to watch it even when I was running a broadcast and publishing empire. Helps that I haven't slept since 1982, but still.

I am definitely the Miranda of the group. Career comes first, no patience for anyone trying to tie me down.

Seriously, I need to host another show. What do people without shows do? I've written three operas and a whole series of sexy novels under the pseudonym "E. L. James." I've learned four languages. How do you fill the hours in the day?

So if I'm Miranda, Hillary is Carrie, and Gwyneth is Charlotte, that makes Beyoncé . . . Samantha? That doesn't make sense. Beyoncé, you're not a Samantha, are you?

O

February 18, 2010

TO: The Fun Four
FROM: Beyoncé
RE: Fun question

I AM NOT SAMANTHA. I AM SHIVA. I AM THE DESTROYER AND THE TRANSFORMER. I AM LIMITLESS, TRANSCENDENT, FORMLESS, AND

ETERNAL. I WEAR FIVE SNAKES AND A GARLAND OF SKULLS AS ORNAMENTATION.

I HAVE WATCHED THE SHOW A FEW TIMES.

OPWYNBEYLARY.
OPWYNBEYLARY.
OPWYNBEYLARY.

BEY

TO: The Fun Four
FROM: HRC
RE: Fun question

Hm. Beyoncé, I don't *think* that Shiva is one of the four main characters on that show?

TO: The Fun Four
FROM: Beyoncé
RE: Fun question

I AM NOT BOUND BY TELEVISION SCRIPTS.

OUR NEXT GATHERING SHALL BE IN MY UNDERSEA FORTRESS. MY ROBOTS WILL COME FOR YOU WHEN IT IS TIME. ALL WILL BE KNOWN ALL WILL BE KNOWN ALL WILL BE KNOWN.

BRING BOARD GAMES.

OPWYNBEYLARY.

BEYONCÉ

★ ★ ★

February 23, 2010

TO: HRC
FROM: Bill
Subject: Interesting

You know who's a much better skier than you'd think?
Cher.

You know who's not as good as you'd think? Joe
Montana.

Anyway, Aspen is fine. Hope you're having fun thinking
about the Middle East.

B

March 23, 2010

TO: HRC
FROM: Barack Obama
Subject: Thank you

Hillary,

Today, as you know, I signed the Affordable Care Act into law. It's a great relief to finally complete this long, exhausting process and sign off on the most significant piece of health care reform legislation this country has ever seen. The Affordable Care Act will see many challenges from our colleagues in the Republican Party, but I am confident that today we made America better.

And I just wanted to say thanks. Thank you for attempting to pass health care reform way back in 1993, back when you were First Lady and I was teaching constitutional law at the University of Chicago. I can imagine it wasn't easy to have such a high-profile failure, in spite of all your hard work. Please know that I respect the bravery you displayed in letting your tortured efforts play out so publicly and in such an embarrassing fashion.

Because it really made the ACA look pretty sharp and cohesive by comparison all these years later. And if your plan had passed, my plan might never have happened. And I love my plan. Kaboom. Signed into law. Health care reform. Who just signed it? I just signed it. Slammo.

B

TO: Chelsea
FROM: HRC
Subject: wedding

Hi honey,

Had an idea for centerpieces. I was thinking an array of wildflowers, roses, eucalyptus, and chrysanthemums all surrounding some small surveys. Golf pencils nearby. The surveys would be about what people would think if I ran for President in 2016, how much they would be willing to donate, to raise from their friends, etc. And really it would be all about you because you grew up in the White House, you see? It's not about me at all! I already have these surveys printed.

Mom

April 16, 2010

TO: HRC
FROM: Chelsea
RE: wedding

No.

★ ★ ★

April 19, 2010

TO: HRC
FROM: Ruth Bader Ginsburg
Subject: Bummer!

Hillary!

First I hear you might be taking the SCOTUS vacancy
left by Stevens, THEN I hear you're not taking it after all!
Bummer!

I'm going to keep telling Scalia and Thomas that I've heard
you ARE coming. It makes them somehow cry with sadness
and anger at the same time. Really a lot of fun to watch
when we're in chambers.

Paintball this weekend?

April 19, 2010

TO: Ruth Bader Ginsburg
FROM: HRC
RE: Bummer!

Damn right, paintball. You and Sotomayor are going down.

★   ★   ★

May 1, 2010

TO: Chelsea
FROM: HRC
Subject: Your wedding!

Oh honey, I can't believe it's only a couple of months away now! Wondering if I could make a quick addition to the guest list. I KNOW we said no more additions but this would mean so much to me. I just want to include the foreign ministers from Pakistan, Tajikistan, Australia, Ecuador, Uruguay, Greece, Liberia, and Chad. And each with a plus one, of course. Plus three for Chad.

It would be a tremendous service to your country. Could be good for your career.

So I'll assume it's a yes, okay?

May 1, 2010

TO: HRC
FROM: Chelsea
RE: Your wedding!

No.

June 20, 2010

TO: HRC
FROM: Prince of AFRICA
Subject: Your Urgent help

DEAR FRIEND,

PLEASE DO NOT BE ALARMED TO HEAR FROM ME. A FRIEND
THAT WE BOTH HAVE HAS TOLD ME TAHT YOU ARE A PERSON
TO BE TRUTSED IN THE FIELD OF GLOBAL SECURITY. MY NAME
IS ABBAH AND I AM THE ONLY SON OF GENERAL FATHER WHO
WAS MY FATHER. HE HAS BEEN KILLED BY THE REBELS IN MY
HOME COUNTRY WHICH IS IN AFRICA THE EXACT PLACE IS
NOT IPMORTANT RIGHT NOW.

IN THE BANK IN THE CAPITAL CITY OF THE COUNTRY IS $320
MILLION DOLLARS WHICH I CAN ONLY ACCES BY GOING
THROUGH THE AMERICA BANKS. I NEED CONTACT WITH AN
AMERICA AND YOUR BANK ACCOUNT INFORMATION. FOR
THIS I GIVE YOU 30%.

ALSO IS THEIS SERIOUSLY THE E-MAIL FOR MRS. CLINTON?
HELLO! PLEASE HELP! I GOT THIS E-MAIL ADDRESS FROM JOE
BIDEN.

★   ★   ★

July 3, 2010

TO: HRC
FROM: Bill
Subject: For future reference

I don't know when or if this will come up for you, but just so you know:

Wilford Brimley has the best hot tub I've ever been in.

Lady Gaga has some really interesting ideas on foreign trade.

George Clooney can eat ten deviled eggs in one sitting.

Talk soon!

Bill

July 6, 2010

TO: HRC
FROM: HRC
Subject: Note to Self: Hair

Sick of media attention on my hairstyle.

Was sick of it in '92, sick of it constantly since then, sick of it now.

Idea: shave head

PRO—by ending hair, end discussion of hairstyle
CON—would likely make me look like supervillain

PRO—could do better things with time normally spent doing hair
CON—sunburn, especially on foreign trips

PRO—could convey image of power and confidence like Michael Jordan
CON—could convey different image if I look like that Heaven's Gate cult leader

PRO—would look totally awesome with wrap-around sunglasses
CON—might look like a Q-tip denuded of cotton

Conclusion: no action yet, keep it in mind.

July 10, 2010

TO: HRC
FROM: Lance of Cleveland
Subject: Pakistan trip

Mrs. Clinton,

Pakistan is a complicated place and, as such, creates significant and exciting challenges in the field of pantsuits. I'm thinking we use a gray base to denote how Pakistan always seems to exist in that kind of in-between zone. Like, yes, they will cooperate or appear to cooperate with our government, but at the same time, they've always kind of had that "harboring terrorists" thing going, which is problematic.

I've considered the idea of having little toy-army-guy-size terrorist figures "harbored" in secret pockets around the pantsuit, but I'm worried the bulges would look odd and invite questions. I would like to add some of those spinning hypnosis disks on the shoulders to denote how confusing and disorienting Pakistan could be.

Lance of Cleveland

P.S. I must admit that I'm getting a little frustrated with your refusal to try some of my more bold and showy pantsuit designs. I realize you are a diplomat first and foremost, but couldn't you be a diplomat with whimsy and pizzazz?

★   ★   ★

July 11, 2010

TO: HRC
FROM: LeBron James
Subject: My decision

Hey, I announced on national television that I was "taking my talents to South Beach" and leaving Cleveland for the Miami Heat and now everyone hates me! I'm despised by all of Cleveland! They're burning my jersey there. I'm looking forward to playing in Miami but I don't think I can ever go home again.

Wait a minute.

You're from Chicago, aren't you? Did you engineer this whole thing, wipe out all the good will I have in Cleveland, make me a pariah, just so that the Bulls wouldn't have to play against me as often? That is low, Hillary Clinton.

July 11, 2010

TO: LeBron James
FROM: HRC
RE: My decision

Have fun in Miami!

Go Bulls!

HRC

July 30, 2010

TO: Chelsea
FROM: HRC
Subject: Tomorrow

My darling Chelsea. I am so excited for you and Marc and your big day tomorrow.

Hypothetically, if Lance of Cleveland (my pantsuit guy) designed a wedding day pantsuit that subliminally spelled out—very subtly, very tastefully—"2016," would you be okay with that? I don't think it would be obtrusive in any way and it would mean a lot to me.

What do you think?

August 1, 2010

TO: Chelsea
FROM: HRC
Subject: Congratulations

Chelsea,

It was a wonderful wedding. I love you both so much.

I did think it was funny when you brought out the Prince impersonator to dance with me at the reception. A great joke! I want you to know that I was not fooled for a moment. I knew it wasn't the real thing. The only reason I cried, screamed, and shouted, "I love you, Your Purple Majesty!" the whole time was that I was very moved by the wedding ceremony.

Mom

August 24, 2010

TO: HRC
FROM: Huma Abedin
Subject: Yoga

Hey,

As you know, we've been bringing in a yoga instructor every Wednesday at 5pm for the past few weeks. A lot of us are really loving it. It's good exercise, it's RELAXING, which we all need, and it's fun too. It would mean so much to the staff if you joined us for class tomorrow. As a staff member, I would be inspired. And as your friend, I think it would do you some good to take a minute to be calm and centered.

See you there?

Huma

August 24, 2010

TO: Huma Abedin, Lance of Cleveland
FROM: HRC
RE: Yoga

One class. Lance?

August 24, 2010

TO: Huma Abedin, HRC
FROM: Lance of Cleveland
RE: Yoga

On it!

TO: HRC
FROM: Huma Abedin
RE: Yoga

First of all, THANK YOU for joining us yesterday!

I talked with the instructor. She and I had some ideas on how you might get even more out of it.

- Maybe next time don't bring a laptop? You might have more success with the poses.

- Also, it's good to be friendly but maybe don't constantly greet all other participants.

- Yoga isn't a competition so there's no need to ask if you "won" after each pose.

The pantsuit looked great, though!

Hope to see you again!

Huma

★ ★ ★

October 4, 2010

TO: HRC
FROM: Barack Obama
Subject: 2012 VP nonsense

Hillary,

Just want to make you aware of some ridiculous rumors going around. We're pretty sure that next month's midterm elections are going to be brutal for us. Might lose the House, could lose the Senate. Gonna be bleak. That has led some people to speculate that I'm going to switch you and Biden, and have you as my running mate, Joe at State.

Obviously, this is complete hogwash. Sure, you're a savvy veteran; you know where the bodies are buried (figuratively, not literally) (I think); and even though you have a lot of enemies, you have even more friends. But to make that switch would smell of desperation. Right? I mean, we shouldn't even consider doing this. Right?

Barack

October 4, 2010

TO: Barack Obama
FROM: HRC
RE: 2012 VP nonsense

We should ABSOLUTELY NOT do this. I'm happy at State; it would look desperate; and, no matter what happens in the midterms, 2012 is a long way away.

I mean, yes, you and I have formed a great relationship, gradually moving from rivals to enemies to colleagues to genuine friends and the third-best beach volleyball team at the highly classified Supreme Court basement tournaments. And of course, it would

63

position me perfectly to run in 2016. I could coast right into the White House because I wouldn't be as completely tone-deaf as Gore was in 2000.

But no, it's wrong. We shouldn't even consider dumping Biden for me.

Right?

H

October 5, 2010

TO: HRC, Barack Obama
FROM: Joe Biden
RE: 2012 VP nonsense

I don't know, you guys. Might be fun! I love foreign policy and traveling around on planes and stuff. And frankly, this whole Naval Observatory business is for the birds. You can't see the Navy at all!

JB

October 5, 2010

TO: Joe Biden
FROM: Barack Obama
CC: HRC
RE: 2012 VP nonsense

Biden, I swear to God I do not know how you get on these e-mails but you need to stop. It's pretty messed up.

TO: Huma Abedin
FROM: HRC
Subject: Kids' Korner on website

I'm sure a lot of kids visit the State Department website every day because kids love global diplomacy issues, everyone knows that. But I thought it might be fun to also have a special section of the site with content that kids know is just for them. We could have games, puzzles, fun tips on how to stage make-believe peace treaty agreements between violent warring factions in their neighborhood, that kind of thing.

And I know the kids will want to hear a lot from me. So I've put together some short book reviews that are fun and helpful.

GREEN EGGS AND HAM—Insultingly simplistic take on the complex art of negotiation. One party irrationally and aggressively insists that the other partake of a disgusting food. The second party is intransigent in his refusal. The impasse continues until the second party is, unrealistically, won over. This book is useless to kids.

GOOD NIGHT MOON—Demonstrates the comfort a person/ rabbit can have with the surveillance state. Should the hero wish the ever-watching Moon good night or try to actually prevent it from getting into the house? More pertinent than ever.

WHERE THE WILD THINGS ARE—This "classic" presents a xenophobic worldview where all places other than one's own home are full of "wild things" who wish to eat you up. Furthering the colonialist mind-set, the white male interloper becomes king of this wild place despite having no qualifications or cultural understanding. Dangerous.

CHARLIE AND THE CHOCOLATE FACTORY—Secretive owner/operator of an unregulated factory employs slave labor to create product that leads to obesity among children. Avoid.

THE GIVING TREE—Bleak but ultimately honest look at the unfettered destruction of nature by humans. Also tells of the frustration and humiliation that is inextricably linked to love.

What do you think? Kids will love it, right?

H

November 10, 2010

TO: HRC
FROM: Huma Abedin
Subject: Something fun

Hi,

You might have noticed something unusual in your office this morning. Some lobbyists for the video game industry dropped off a new Xbox 360 and the game Call of Duty: Black Ops. It's supposed to be a really great game although pretty violent.

Anyway, if you need to blow off some steam, give it a go.

November 10, 2010

TO: Huma Abedin
FROM: HRC
RE: Something fun

Thanks. I'm sure any game like this is beyond my capabilities. The last game I played with any real concentration was Ms. Pac-Man but I ultimately got frustrated with how she felt a need to wear lipstick and I worried the ghosts didn't take her seriously.

I doubt I'll get to this one.

November 11, 2010

TO: Secretary Robert Gates
FROM: HRC
Subject: Be prepared

Bob,

I've been playing this video game called Call of Duty: Black Ops all night. As a result, the game is starting to feel like reality and all the elements of the actual world we live in have begun to fall away. And now I'm worried about you.

You see, there's part of the game where Nazi zombies have invaded the Pentagon and you have to defeat them playing as either JFK, Nixon, Castro, or Robert McNamara. I know it sounds crazy, but you wouldn't believe how realistic this thing is. Anyway, watch out for Nazis, okay, Bob?

HRC

November 11, 2010

TO: HRC
FROM: Secretary Robert Gates
RE: Be prepared

Okay. I'll be on the lookout for Nazi zombies.

Thanks.

★ ★ ★

TO: Barack Obama
FROM: HRC
Subject: Cuba

So I've been playing Call of Duty: Black Ops for a few days now and it is FANTASTIC. The excitement! The action! The weapons! I LOVE THIS GAME!

There's this part of it where you battle Nazi zombies at the Pentagon and you can play as Fidel Castro. I've been doing that for several hours today and it's really made me feel better about him. Like it's not even his country but he's there fighting the Nazi zombies anyway.

My point is: maybe we should discreetly work toward normalizing relations with Cuba. The Cold War and the Cuban Missile Crisis were a long time ago.

I think I'm going to set things in motion so that in, oh, I don't know, 2015, we could have an opening of the borders and get things to a better place. And when that happens, no one will know that it was all because of CALL OF DUTY: BLACK OPS, THE GREATEST GAME IN THE WORLD.

HRC

★ ★ ★

TO: HRC
FROM: Huma Abedin
Subject: Xbox

I've taken the Xbox away and the game as well.

Confidentially, the staff has become uncomfortable with how much time you were spending playing it. The sounds of explosions were distracting and upsetting. It also bothered people to have the Secretary of State yelling, "DIE! DIE! DIE, YOU NAZI SCUM!," especially when there were visitors in the building.

I can get you some Sudoku books if you like.

Huma

TO: HRC
FROM: Vince Gilligan
Subject: Breaking Bad—Season 4

Madam Secretary,

I hope you are well. As you know, Breaking Bad has been picked up for another season. Fans are already super excited about the premiere coming this spring. The more challenging news is that our show, the show you and I created together, needs your help. Truth be told, we all have total writer's block. Haven't written a word, haven't shot a frame.

We're in trouble and we need you.

Yes, I know that you are very busy with your duties, and I understand that those things are way more important than a TV show.

In the show, Walter and Jesse are in pretty deep against the drug kingpin Gus Fring. He wants to kill them but he needs them. They want to escape from him but they can't. It's all fine for a while but HOW CAN WE POSSIBLY SUSTAIN THAT? Sorry. A little panicky.

Help?

TO: Vince Gilligan
FROM: HRC
RE: Breaking Bad—Season 4

Vince,

First thing: no one can know I'm the creative force behind Breaking Bad. It's too brutal of a show. I don't need pundits and the foreign press knowing that my mind can work that way.

Second, I'm a little too busy right now preparing for an economic summit in Kazakhstan to come up with a new season of Breaking Bad.

But fine. I got an idea where Walt convinces Hector Salamanca to be a suicide bomb and blow up Fring. Then we pan back and see Fring but half his flesh has been blown off his body. That's off the top of my head. I'll sketch out the season on the plane.

HRC

November 19, 2010

TO: HRC
FROM: Vince Gilligan
RE: Breaking Bad—Season 4

Wow. That's really hardcore. I mean, I'm horrified even thinking about that. You have that in your imagination? And you're going to be the leader of the free world? Wow. Okay. I need to go watch some cartoons now to detox.

But thanks.

★ ★ ★

November 30, 2010

TO: State Department Staff
FROM: HRC
Subject: Leaks

Hi everyone.

Obviously, we're in heavy damage-control mode right now with the release of all these leaked documents. They contain a lot of things we said amongst ourselves about other countries. We talked about Turkey being "lost in neo-Ottoman Islamist fantasies," for instance. I'll grant you, that's a pretty sick burn, but it's embarrassing for other nations to hear our catty gossip.

To the best of my knowledge, the following things we've said about other countries have not yet been leaked so let's make sure that everything along these lines is deleted immediately:

- England is a bunch of snobs and Benedict Cumberbatch is overrated.

- Chad sounds like a frat guy's name and not a country's name.

- Canada has bad posture.

- Belgium clearly prefers Sammy Hagar over David Lee Roth.

- Argentina is bad at flossing.

- Pakistan cheats at Trivial Pursuit.

- Australia is always regifting things and it's kind of tacky.

- Sweden has poorly trained dogs.

- New Zealand has lousy salad bars.

- Malaysia has weird chairs.

Again, for anything related to leaks, please get in touch with me through this secret e-mail that no one knows about and that can never be hacked into and leaked out to the public, causing embarrassment.

HRC

November 30, 2010

TO: HRC
FROM: Huma Abedin
RE: Leaks

I have this video of our State Department improv troupe. They're doing a really funny thing about how El Salvador is bad at drawing animals and how Azerbaijan doesn't know how to open jars.

November 30, 2010

TO: Huma Abedin
FROM: HRC
RE: Leaks

Destroy it. Destroy it now.

December 2, 2010

TO: HRC
FROM: Bill
Subject: Kazakhstan trip

Hi honey,

Hope you're enjoying Kazakhstan. I've been walking around the foundation offices saying to everyone, "You know who's in Kazakhstan? MY WIIIIIIIFE!" Like Borat! Everyone thinks it's really funny. It never gets old! Wait, do you think they're just laughing to be nice to me?

Nah, it's hysterical! MY WIIIIIIIIIFE! MY WIIIIIIIIIIFE! MY WIIIIIIIIFE!

Anyway, have fun. I'm going snowshoeing with Martin Scorsese and all the guys from Entourage.

Bill

December 10, 2010

TO: Lance of Cleveland
FROM: HRC
Subject: Holiday parties

Holiday season is coming up and I want to make sure I'm ready. Here's what I'll need:

- tasteful red and green pantsuit

- more red than green pantsuit

- more green than red pantsuit

- "tacky sweater" pantsuit for one of those silly tacky sweater parties. Should be garish but not undignified, as I have a public image to think about. I want it to be the tackiest thing at the party—I like to win—but also appropriate for a head of state. Embarrassingly awful but not embarrassing? Does that make sense?

HRC

December 10, 2010

TO: HRC
FROM: Lance of Cleveland
RE: Holiday parties

Am I to take it from this e-mail that you are rejecting the Mrs. Claus pantsuit I presented last week? The one that I spent weeks and weeks working on? I urge you to reconsider it one more time.

TO: Lance of Cleveland
FROM: HRC
RE: Holiday parties

Of course I did! I am one of the most important and powerful diplomats in the world. What I do has a major impact on war and peace and economies around the world. I AM NOT MOTHERF'ING MRS. CLAUS. For God's sake, what kind of person is she, anyway? Her husband is an international hero and she, what, makes cookies? Sweeps up around their desolate polar cabin? No, that is not the image I want to convey.

TO: HRC
FROM: Lance of Cleveland
RE: Holiday parties

I did NOT take this job to be yelled at, MA'AM. I can walk into any pantsuit corporation in the world and name my own salary. I am working for you because I care about our country and the pantsuits with which it represents itself.

But perhaps I am no longer wanted.

TO: Lance of Cleveland
FROM: HRC
RE: Holiday parties

Not if you're going to make me pantsuits like that, you aren't! I'm the boss here, pal. No more Mrs. Claus pantsuits. No more Rudolph or Frosty pantsuits either (yes, I saw your sketches). And

I've managed to not talk about your proposed Thanksgiving turkey pantsuit but I am still very angry about it.

Watch your step.

December 10, 2010

TO: HRC
FROM: Lance of Cleveland
RE: Holiday parties

How about YOU watch my step? My steps as I walk out of here! I got offers from Pelosi, Claire McCaskill, a LOT of people.

December 11, 2010

TO: Huma Abedin
FROM: HRC
Subject: Quick question

How are you at making pantsuits? Lance of Cleveland is no longer with us.

December 11, 2010

TO: HRC
FROM: Huma Abedin
RE: Quick question

No longer with us? Like fired or quit or has been killed?

December 11, 2010

TO: Huma Abedin
FROM: HRC
RE: Quick question

Let's see how it plays out.

December 18, 2010

TO: Mr. Pantsuit
FROM: HRC
Subject: Shot in the dark

Gentlemen,

When I began this position as Secretary of State, I decided to go with a different pantsuit resource. I realize only now that this was a mistake.

I am sorry.

I now find myself without dedicated pantsuit personnel and the holiday season is well underway.

Would you have me back? Would you make me pantsuits again?

Mrs. Clinton

December 18, 2010

TO: HRC
FROM: Mr. Pantsuit
RE: Shot in the dark

A THOUSAND TIMES YES.

Mrs. Clinton, we never stopped working for you. Over the last two years, we have continued to make you pantsuits for every occasion: fancy Washington gala, overseas trip to war-torn region, just everyday, around-the-house pantsuiting. We knew you would not take them so, upon completing each pantsuit, we would simply display it in our office and gaze upon it in silent contemplation for a few hours. Times like these, we were thankful we had that eerily lifelike wax statue of you built. "Hillary 2" looks great in these pantsuits.

We still haven't had other customers. We don't really want them. We turn them away, actually. We are quite broke. Our office is really just an abandoned warehouse space down by the docks. We get in by climbing through a broken window. We get cut by the glass pretty often. We've all grown quite thin and raggedy.

But we kept our machines and our fabric and our wax statue and our commitment. And our e-mail address! So glad to hear from you.

We'll be over in 20 minutes with 50 pantsuits to choose from.

Thank you.

★ ★ ★ ★ ★ ★ ★ ★ ★

2011

★ ★ ★ ★ ★ ★ ★ ★ ★

TO: Huma Abedin
FROM: HRC
Subject: Middle East trip

Hey,

So we have Yemen, Oman, United Arab Emirates, and Qatar on this trip coming up. These are cultures that are generally pretty primitive in terms of human rights, women's rights, and social issues in general. It is such a contrast to our own culture of free expression, where charismatic and attractive artists can really express themselves and draw people to them, sometimes hypnotically.

Here's my idea: what if we bring some important American artist with us? Like a musician who can really bring everyone together? Somebody young but not all that young? Somebody iconic, maybe who has played the Super Bowl. Wouldn't that be great?

January 3, 2011

TO: HRC
FROM: Huma Abedin
RE: Middle East trip

We. Can't. Get. Prince.

★   ★   ★

TO: HRC
FROM: Shonda Rhimes
Subject: "Scandal"

Hello Mrs. Clinton,

I received your e-mail from Vince Gilligan. And then, weirdest thing, Joe Biden sent it to me as well, and I don't even know Joe Biden. Anyway, I hope it's okay to reach you here.

I'm a television producer, probably best known for creating the shows Grey's Anatomy and Private Practice. I'm working on a new show, tentatively called Scandal, about life inside Washington, D.C. Given my track record, there are a lot of expectations for this show and I must admit I'm struggling.

Both Vince and Chris told me that besides being the country's top diplomat and one of the world's most-admired women, you are a top-notch "fixer" of movies and TV shows.

What do you think the show should focus on? What would YOU really like to see from a show like this?

Shonda

TO: Shonda Rhimes
FROM: HRC
RE: "Scandal"

Hi Shonda,

The project sounds fascinating but I really do far, far too much secret script-doctoring as it is. I've had to pull those Transformer movies out of the fire recently, which took a whole lot of time that I did not have. So I'm afraid I couldn't really help you with this.

That being said, the obvious path is to place someone unexpected in the leading role. Namely, a strong and powerful woman who knows everything and everyone in Washington and has the skills and intelligence to scheme her way to absolute power. Someone who is admired and feared in equal measure.

But again, far too busy. Can't help you. I'll have Huma set up a series of appointments with you over the next few months to talk about the story, which I'm much too busy to help you with.

Hillary

February 2, 2011

TO: Barack Obama
FROM: HRC
Subject: Egypt

Barack,

Obviously, the situation on the ground in Cairo is changing fast.
A few days ago, we were still supporting President Mubarak amid
the rising protests. Just recently, we took a harder stance and
condemned Mubarak's blocking of the Internet within his country.
It's clear that unless something dramatic and unexpected comes
about to slow down the protests, Mubarak is on his way out. Many
of us will not be sad to see this oppressive head of state go.

However, I don't think that installing me as temporary President
of Egypt is the correct response. Yes, I'm the smartest, most
respected, and most capable leader on the planet who does not
officially have a country to lead. Yes, I know a great deal about
Egypt and could learn even more. And yes, of course, such a move
could drag the entire region into a century where women are
respected as equals to men. But I am so busy with my current job
and would not want to leave my staff at this point because we've
grown quite close.

Hillary

February 2, 2011

TO: HRC
FROM: Barack Obama
RE: Egypt

I'm confused. Who said anything about you becoming
temporary President of Egypt?

Barack

THE DELETED E-MAILS OF HILLARY CLINTON

February 2, 2011

TO: Barack Obama
FROM: HRC
RE: Egypt

Well, exactly. We should not do it despite how much stability it would instantly bring to the region. And even though I would finally get the power that we all agree I richly deserve, this is neither the time nor the place.

It's not even my call to make, really. If you insisted I take over Egypt, I couldn't refuse since I serve at the pleasure of the President. I'm just here to advise you that I think it's probably not a good idea. I'm pretty sure we have discussed it, though. I think you suggested it.

Hillary

February 2, 2011

TO: HRC
FROM: Barack Obama
RE: Egypt

Just . . . keep me updated on Egypt, okay? No matter who's running it. Which is not you.

Barack

February 20, 2011

TO: HRC
FROM: Bill
Subject: Arab Spring

Honey,

I am just watching all this stuff go down across the Arab world and it just looks tough. We need to be supporting democracy and freedom while also establishing stable governments so that these regions don't plunge into anarchy and bloodshed.

At these tense times, I wonder if you could use some support and advice from seasoned, experienced diplomats. I wonder if you're looking for some wisdom from someone who has been dealing with these issues at the highest level for decades.

If so, I hope you find that person. Me, I'm going over to John Fogerty's house to jam out for a while. We're thinking of starting a new band! I think we could get Billy Joel. Have you ever tried Red Bull?

Bill

★   ★   ★

March 5, 2011

TO: HRC
FROM: Barack Obama
Subject: Libya

Just so you know, I don't want you taking over Libya either.

March 5, 2011

TO: Barack Obama
FROM: HRC
RE: Libya

Don't want it. Way too messy.

As we discussed, I'm gathering international support to authorize military intervention in Libya in case we reach a point when Gaddafi might start attacking his own people. Hopefully we won't need it but better to be prepared.

Yep, a carefully planned approach to everything in Libya is the way to go. Not only is it the most prudent course, it also means that the Republicans can never come after me for something that might happen in Libya that I had very little to do with.

Hillary

★ ★ ★

TO: Campaign Staff
FROM: HRC
Subject: Lessons learned

Hi all,

Thanks for being on this list of people who could potentially get involved in a 2016 presidential run, in case I make the decision to run at some point. Again, I haven't decided whether to do that and I haven't even had much time to think about it!

One of the things that's been keeping me busy lately is the Arab Spring, the protests going on all over the Arab world that have led to new leadership in several countries. The people who now serve in the highest offices in those countries generally didn't get there through $10,000-a-plate fund-raisers or Super PACs or expensive television commercials. They did it two ways: social media and street protests. And it worked!

So maybe for 2016 we take a look at that. Let's get a strong presence on Facebook, Twitter, Pinterest, and whatever else emerges between now and then. Let's also plan to have thousands of angry young people pour into the street in every major city and create violent though non-fatal protests demanding that I become President. Angry mobs! Students who never seem to go to class! If those go well enough, we wouldn't even really need an election. We'd have it, to be polite, but everyone would know the score by then.

It's campaign reform, kind of.

Really, I'm just spitballing here. Trying to use my knowledge and experience for future projects.

Hillary

March 16, 2011

TO: Campaign Staff
FROM: HRC
RE: Lessons learned

How come no one ever writes back on these things?

March 19, 2011

TO: HRC
FROM: Sarah Palin
Subject: Hello there!

Hi Hillary,

I saw your interview on Wolf Blitzer that you wouldn't want to be the Secretary of State after Barak gets elected a second time if he does get elected a second time because maybe he won't because I might beat him in the president picking contest election.

So it got me to wondering: maybe I could be the Secretary of State instead of you because then you would be done with that job and I could put in an application for it to be me instead of you or something. Got it? Okay!

Which state is it?

Okay then, hope you're well. Call me! I can't find my phone.

Sarah

March 21, 2011

TO: Sarah Palin
FROM: HRC
RE: Hello there!

Hello Sarah,

I'm having my staff send you some basic pamphlets on how our system of government works. I'm also guessing that if President Obama needed to replace me, he would likely choose someone with diplomatic experience, someone who shared many or most of his core beliefs, and someone who wasn't you.

Best of luck to you.

Hillary

April 20, 2011

TO: HRC
FROM: HRC
Subject: Note to Self—18 million cracks

Concession speech given in 2008 race referenced 18 million cracks in glass ceiling. 18 million voters who helped me almost ALMOST bust up the highest, hardest glass ceiling and send a woman to the White House for reasons other than marriage. People really responded to that 18 million cracks line.

Might be good to use best lines earlier in a campaign instead of after campaign is dead.

But how to leverage success of the 18 million cracks idea in possible future campaign?

- Hillary Cracks. Everyone who supports campaign gets a nickname. They're "Cracks." "Come celebrate our Iowa victory with your fellow Cracks."

- Give people a miniature cracked ceiling for donating.

- Construct intricate cracked ceiling canopy for all speaking appearances (danger of glass shards raining down on audience, cutting them severely?).

- Fund-raiser where if you donate you get to take a whack at a piece of reinforced Plexiglas to try to crack it. Risk: could be dangerous if it cracks, depressing if it does not.

- Give out free jagged glass shards to donors as a thank-you gift. Illegal to send through mail though?

- Soft-edged glass pieces to rain down from ceiling at convention when I'm the nominee? Might be terrifying.

Keep thinking, Hillary.

HRC

★　★　★

May 1, 2011

TO: The Fun Four
FROM: HRC
Subject: International security

Ladies,

Osama bin Laden was located and killed. The world is a safer place because of that. I thank you, and your country thanks you as well, for all your work leading up to the success of this mission.

At this crucial moment when the eyes of the world are upon us, it is very important that your efforts, while valuable, remain a secret. If people were to find out how skilled and resourceful you are, in addition to how famous and popular you are, the very balance of world power could tilt. And it is not time for that yet.

Oprah, this means no one can learn how you, as a master of disguises, went undercover in Pakistan, disguising yourself as a local and gathering intelligence that pointed us toward Osama's compound in Abbottabad.

Gwyneth, we all knew you had a mastery of skin lotions and yoga positions, but nobody expected that you would be a world-class communications expert as well. How you coordinated global spy satellites from the ground in Pakistan using only a hot glue gun and some quinoa, well, I'll never fully understand but will always appreciate.

And Beyoncé, your skilled instruction to Seal Team 6 on exactly how to carry out the operation was indispensable. Many members of that team remarked how it had seemed like you had carried out similar missions many times before, but they were too frightened of you to bring that up.

Anyway, we got him.

And as far as the world knows, Oprah was spending quiet time at home, Gwyneth was at a meditation retreat, and Beyoncé was "in the studio." Let's keep it that way.

Opwynbeylary, my sisters. Opwynbeylary.

Hills

★ ★ ★

May 11, 2011

TO: HRC
FROM: Mr. Pantsuit
Subject: New ideas

Hello Mrs. Clinton!

Congratulations to you and the entire administration
on bin Laden. We had some new ideas for pantsuits to
celebrate this occasion and wanted to run them by you.

We were thinking a bright red, white, and blue ensemble
with a neon American flag on the back. It would represent
America. Then there would be additional lights of little
terrorists running away from the flag because they know
that America means business and not to mess with us.

You like?

95

TO: Mr. Pantsuit
FROM: HRC
RE: New ideas

No. Just make the pantsuits look neutral and professional. Earth tones. Browns. No neon. Never any neon. Good Lord.

HRC

★   ★   ★

TO: (names hidden)
FROM: Joe Biden
Subject: You must forward this letter!

THIS IS NOT A JOKE!

IF YOU FORWARD THIS MESSAGE ON TO TEN OF YOUR FRIENDS BY MIDNIGHT TOMORROW YOU WILL HAVE GREAT SUCCESS! WEALTH! LOVE! POWER! HAPPINESS!!!

IF YOU DON'T FORWARD IT, TERRIBLE THINGS WILL HAPPEN TO YOU!

THIS HAS BEEN INVESTIGATED BY SCIENCE AND IT IS TRUE!

IT IS VERY IMPORTANT!!!!!!!!!!!!!!!!!!!!!!!!!!

Hey guys, it's Joe. This sounded crazy but I thought what the heck.

May 20, 2011

TO: (names hidden)
FROM: George W. Bush
RE: You must forward this letter!

The evidence on this doesn't seem to really be all there but I'll go ahead and charge ahead with it anyway.

Message forwarded. Mission accomplished.

May 20, 2011

TO: (names hidden)
FROM: Dick Cheney
RE: You must forward this letter!

Dammit, Biden! Stop using the official vice-presidential computers for this kind of junk! By the way, I'm not still hiding in the vice-presidential bunker but just don't come in here ever, okay? I mean there. Don't come in there.

May 20, 2011

TO: (names hidden)
FROM: John McCain
RE: You must forward this letter!

This thing is for real, folks. I didn't forward it when I got it back in '08 and I ended up losing an election to a guy with the middle name Hussein.

TO: (names hidden)
FROM: Mitt Romney
RE: You must forward this letter!

Sounds neat! I'll do it!

Wait, is this witchcraft?

TO: (names hidden)
FROM: HRC
RE: You must forward this letter!

Would everyone please stop hitting Reply All on this stupid thing?

TO: (names hidden)
FROM: Sarah Palin
RE: You must forward this letter!

How do you Reply All on an e-mail?

TO: (names hidden)
FROM: HRC
RE: You must forward this letter!

You just di—oh, never mind.

★ ★ ★

THE DELETED E-MAILS OF HILLARY CLINTON

June 6, 2011

TO: HRC
FROM: Huma Abedin
Subject: advice

Hi,

Well, apparently Anthony lied to me. The "Weiner Sexting Scandal" is all true and I am devastated. You are my boss but you are also my friend. Wondering if you have any advice on how I could handle this going forward.

Huma

June 6, 2011

TO: Huma Abedin
FROM: HRC
RE: advice

Been there. Here's what you do.

- Don't stand next to him at the press conference.

- Don't go on Barbara Walters and talk about how you still love him.

- Begin a slow build to becoming one of the most powerful people on the planet.

- Get packed for our trip to Africa and let's get drunk on the plane.

Hillary

P.S. Please, for the love of everything in this world, do not give your husband my e-mail.

★ ★ ★

June 22, 2011

TO: Huma Abedin
FROM: HRC
Subject: website idea

You know, so many funny things happen here at our department and as I travel around the world. Maybe we should have a section of the website called HILLARY-OUS full of funny stories, jokes, and anecdotes that I run across.

And there are so many examples right off the top of my head. Like the time South Korea's foreign minister, Yu Myung-hwan, thought that I was talking about the Mutual Defense Treaty when I was actually talking about the Free Trade Agreement. He was like, "What do tariff levels have to do with border security?" Oh my gosh, we laughed so hard. Through translators.

Then there was the time when I couldn't remember if Azizmo was the name of the President of Tajikistan's wife or the President of Kyrgyzstan's wife! It was very funny. At least at first. Then it almost led to a complete collapse of diplomatic relations with both countries. So we might not want to include that one.

Maybe there can even be fun quizzes like:

WHO'S THE PRESIDENT OF BAHRAIN? (trick question! Bahrain is a unitary parliamentary constitutional monarchy!)

Anyway, there are all sorts of HILLARY-OUS things like that and I'm sure people would enjoy them.

HRC

TO: HRC
FROM: Vladimir Putin
Subject: what I can do

Dearest Mrs. Hillary Clinton America,

Greetings from Russia.

Do you think that I could capture and eat a lion?

By this I mean, do you think that if I went to jungle, and I found lion in the tall grasses, I could grab lion, kill it with my hands, and then eat lion? Not even cut it into meat and cook on stove or anything. Just eat it mouthful by mouthful. Hair, bones, all of it.

I think I could. I think I would not wear shirt while I catch and eat lion.

I am not sure about tiger, but I use lion eating as experience to train for tiger.

Vladimir

July 31, 2011

TO: Vladimir Putin
FROM: HRC
RE: what I can do

Is this a metaphor for some kind of geopolitical threat? Are you trying to intimidate me?

TO: HRC
FROM: Vladimir Putin
RE: what I can do

Oh no. I just sit here and think about it.

My best friend is a shark. I can punch out any robot.

Thank you, Mrs. Hillary Clinton America!

July 31, 2011

TO: Vladimir Putin
FROM: HRC
RE: what I can do

I'm not even going to ask where you got this e-mail address. I already know.

July 31, 2011

TO: HRC, Vladimir Putin
FROM: Joe Biden
RE: what I can do

Hi, everyone!

August 3, 2011

TO: HRC
FROM: Bill
Subject: Russia!

Hi!

Hey, would it be okay with the State Department if I took a quick little trip to Russia? Putin says he's going to wrestle a bear and then eat it. I kinda want to see that.

I mean, it's either that or hang out with Art Garfunkel all weekend. Yawn.

Bill

TO: Simon & Schuster
FROM: HRC
Subject: Young me

Hi book person,

You know, so many books have been written by me and about me that focus exclusively on what I did in Arkansas or as First Lady or in the Senate or even now as Secretary of State. I was thinking it might be fun to do a book about what I was like in my younger years.

Possible chapter ideas:

- How the only Christmas present I wanted at age five was Power and how uncomfortable it made the department store Santa to hear that

- The development of the playground game Crush All Those Who Get in My Way (later banned by nervous administrators)

- Letting the principal of my elementary school believe he was in charge when I alone wielded real power

- Campaigning for Goldwater (yes, it's true!) and how he could have won if he had returned my phone calls

- How I selected the right pantsuit to wear to senior prom

What do you think?

HRC

★ ★ ★

TO: HRC
FROM: Mr. Pantsuit
Subject: UN Meeting

Dear Mrs. Clinton,

It is our understanding that you have some important meetings coming up at the United Nations later this month.

Enclosed please find a sketch of a proposed pantsuit. As you will note, it features the flags of all 193 member states of the UN. In addition, there is a pulsating "trouble spot" on the left shoulder with a faint flag of Palestine. It's there but it's not quite there, you know? Anyway, it's meant to represent the issue of Palestinian statehood and UN recognition, which will be the main subject of these UN meetings.

Should we go ahead and confirm this?

September 4, 2011

TO: Mr. Pantsuit
FROM: HRC
RE: UN Meeting

No. I am actually getting concerned about this trend. Why are you suddenly bringing me these unworkable, impractical, gaudy designs? Is there a new team there?

September 4, 2011

TO: HRC
FROM: Mr. Pantsuit
RE: UN Meeting

In fact, we just hired a new designer! All the better to serve you! His name is Lance of Cleveland. He says if you'll just give his pantsuits a chance, you won't be sorry.

September 4, 2011

TO: Mr. Pantsuit
FROM: HRC
RE: UN Meeting

Fire him. You know what I'm capable of.

HRC

★ ★ ★

TO: HRC
FROM: Vladimir Putin
Subject: Shark and robot challenge

Hello Mrs. Hillary Clinton America,

As you know, I am not President of Russia because constitution does not allow it. So I am Premier instead. Until I get to be President again. This means that all I have to do now is run country instead of running country AND appearing at fancy state events. So I have extra time for lion eating and bear fighting (both successful!).

I have been doing experiment lately. I tie one of my shark friends to each fist and then we try to destroy war robot I built.

Is difficult because I build very good war robot. But sharks are good at biting.

Vladimir

September 13, 2011

TO: Vladimir Putin
FROM: HRC
RE: Shark and robot challenge

Okay. Why are you telling me this?

September 13, 2011

TO: HRC
FROM: Vladimir Putin
RE: Shark and robot challenge

Is good, yes? You are impressed?

I am, how you say, in love with you, Mrs. Hillary Clinton America. I want you to know that if you divorce Bill (who is my dear friend and bet on me against the bear), I will make you very happy with strength and smart and sharks tied onto my arms. You will be glad to have a man who can do this.

September 13, 2011

TO: Vladimir Putin
FROM: HRC
RE: Shark and robot challenge

Mr. Putin, I am flattered by your affections, but I am a married woman. Even if I weren't, it seems problematic for an American Secretary of State and a Russian Premier to be involved. I'm sure you agree.

September 13, 2011

TO: HRC
FROM: Vladimir Putin
RE: Shark and robot challenge

I understand but I am not a man who gives up.

I have several ideas of how we could be together:

- I leave Russia and become American citizen. I settle down and become Premier of some United State no one cares about. Delaware? Utah?

- I invade America and you work for me!

- We both quit our jobs and countries but use our militaries to take over somewhere nice like Argentina and we govern together.

Yes, Mrs. Hillary Clinton America? Yes?

September 13, 2011

TO: Vladimir Putin
FROM: HRC
RE: Shark and robot challenge

No.

TO: Barack Obama
FROM: HRC
Subject: Interesting discovery

Barack,

Okay, so I've been up for the past two nights studying the history of Syrian economic policy in hopes of finding some sort of solution to all the problems over there.

I have been consuming nothing but coffee and Gummi Bears to stay awake. Late last night, could have been this morning, I decided to take a little break just to reset. I couldn't decide whether I wanted to watch a movie or listen to some music, so I did both. I put on a DVD of The Wizard of Oz and a CD of Metallica's Ride the Lightning.

IT TURNS OUT THAT WHEN YOU PLAY THEM BOTH TOGETHER, YOU GET ALL THE ANSWERS.

The song "Fight Fire with Fire" is part of it, and so is the Wicked Witch setting the Scarecrow on fire. Wizard of Oz is all about escaping Kansas and then Metallica has a song called "Escape"!

IT ALL MAKES SENSE!

So the answer in Syria is . . . wait, what was I saying?

OH YEAH, METALLICA AND THE WIZARD OF OZ AND SYRIA, WHAT WE HAVE TO DO IS . . . damn, I lost it again.

I think I better get some sleep.

HRC

★ ★ ★

October 2, 2011

TO: The Fun Four
FROM: HRC
Subject: expansion?

Hi everyone!

Sorry we weren't able to get together last summer. So busy! Let's for sure try to do something this Christmas season, okay?

We've been keeping our group pretty locked down over the last few years. I wonder, however, if we should consider expansion. There are so many great people out there with whom we could potentially have very successful partnerships.

First, I'm wondering if you all are open to this. Second, I have some thoughts on potential nominees:

Meryl Streep—We all know she'll play me in a movie someday and get an Oscar for doing so. I'm interested in getting her in the inner circle so that portrayal could be sympathetic. Secret skill: explosives.

Martha Stewart—Not the star she once was but she did time in prison. So in case we're ever in a situation where the sh*t really goes down, she can take care of herself and protect us. Secret skill: can make a weapon or centerpiece out of anything.

Amy Poehler—She's a star on the rise and she's funny. She's also played me, so could be used as a decoy me. Would be useful in case we're under attack in any potential scenario where we take over the world and bend it to our will, not that that would happen. Secret skill: speaks 12 languages.

Prince—A bit of a stretch considering he's not a woman. But I just think having him around would be a really good idea. Especially on some of those cabin trips to remote locations that we've talked about. Secret skill: super seduction, I bet. I'm just guessing.

Hills

October 2, 2011

TO: The Fun Four
FROM: Oprah
RE: expansion?

First three are pretty good ideas. Fourth one, what?

Other possibility:

Gayle King—My best friend who is so much my BFF that she's become pretty much a second flesh vessel for the soul known as Oprah. Would be convenient.

October 2, 2011

TO: The Fun Four
FROM: Gwyneth
RE: expansion?

I'm afraid I must give a thumbs-down on Prince as well.

Only names I could add to the list:

Serena Williams—Strong, accomplished, confident. Secret skill: is really good at making plants grow. Not the most necessary skill, I grant you, but it's very nice.

Gwyneth Paltrow—Not entirely me, mind you, but a robotic creation that goes by the same name. She's made out of yoga pants, condensed salad, and feelings. Also, she seems to have achieved a level of sentience since she's taken to staggering around the room giving patronizing lifestyle advice to other inanimate objects around the house. I like her.

Gwyneth Paltrow (v. 2–9)—Later iterations of same.

October 2, 2011

TO: The Fun Four
FROM: Beyoncé
RE: expansion?

THERE CAN BE ONLY FOUR. ALL OTHERS WOULD BE DESTROYED. I AM BEYONCÉ. I WOULD DESTROY THEM ALL.

ESPECIALLY PRINCE. WHY DOESN'T HE DO MORE STUFF WITH MORRIS DAY AND THE TIME? OR APOLLONIA? I LOVED THAT.

BEY

★ ★ ★

TO: Huma Abedin
FROM: HRC
Subject: Gaddafi

Well, he's dead. His people have spoken. The world can move on.

I still remember when the United States bombed Libya back in 1986. I'll tell you one thing about the United States: give us a quarter of a century, we'll get our man.

H

★ ★ ★ ★ ★ ★ ★ ★ ★

2012–2013

★ ★ ★ ★ ★ ★ ★ ★ ★

TO: The Fun Four
FROM: Oprah
Subject: Summer plans

First off, Hillary, thanks for sending me all those briefing books on Chinese trade policy dating back to the 19th century. Millions of pages. I loved it. Kept me busy for the whole weekend. This whole not-having-a-show thing is great. I get so much done. I'm building a rocket ship. It should be done tomorrow. Unless I go over to Gayle's house.

Big thing: girlfriends, we need to make a plan for the annual summer retreat! Anyone up for hosting?

O

January 4, 2012

TO: The Fun Four
FROM: Gwyneth
RE: Summer plans

Ooh, I would totally be up for it but I'm having a huge body rebuild done right now! Getting milk injections for my face and organic honey suffused into my spine for freshness, and a guy just sold me what he told me are crushed fairy bodies that I'm getting injected into my scalp with a compressed air gun (supposed to give more bounce). It's keeping me so busy and anesthetized that I just have no time to plan! There's a loud buzzing sound I keep hearing and everything tastes like construction paper. All busy moms should do this!

Gwyneth

January 4, 2012

TO: The Fun Four
FROM: HRC
RE: Summer plans

Oh my goodness, I will absolutely do my best to make summer work. As I have already indicated to the press, this will be my last year serving as Secretary of State, so summer might be busy. But still, I need my girl time. I'll see if Barack can toss me the keys to Camp David for a weekend. It's a lovely facility—peaceful, quiet, great food, and you can hunt actual human beings with rifles and shoot them dead. Ha! Just kidding. They're animatronic mannequins that have been built to skitter through the woods. You can really shoot them, though. It's pretty weird, to be honest with you. Cheney had it put in.

January 4, 2012

TO: The Fun Four
FROM: Beyoncé
RE: Summer plans

HILLARY,

IF YOU ARE ENDING YOUR TIME AS SECRETARY OF STATE, WHAT DOES THIS MEAN FOR OPWYNBEYLARY?! WE HAVE DONE TOO MUCH WORK TO TAKE OVER THE WORLD TO LET THIS OPPORTUNITY GET AWAY. I HAVE SPENT MANY HOURS ON THE CHARTERED TOUR JET DRAWING UP EXTENSIVE SCHEMATICS ON STABILIZING GLOBAL CURRENCY AND QUELLING CIVIC UNREST.

BEY

January 4, 2012

TO: The Fun Four
FROM: HRC
RE: Summer plans

Oh my. Well, I know we talked about world conquest as a possibility, but I saw those conversations as more of a fun bonding idea. A daydream. Beyoncé, were you planning on this being a guaranteed plan? Because I think the rest of us were mostly kidding around.

H

January 4, 2012

TO: The Fun Four
FROM: Beyoncé
RE: Summer plans

BEYONCÉ HAS NO SENSE OF HUMOR. BEYONCÉ IS ALL ABOUT SETTING GOALS AND ACHIEVING THEM.

MAYBE I HAVE TO DO THIS WITHOUT YOU ALL.

BEY

January 5, 2012

TO: Barack Obama
FROM: HRC
Subject: Just to keep on your radar

Hi,

I am contacting you through this, my secret e-mail, so as not to have it on the public record. If the American people knew about this, I don't know what would happen, but I know it would not be good.

For a while now, I've been part of an informal group of friends. Me, Oprah, Gwyneth Paltrow, and Beyoncé. Beyoncé signed on soon after we let Björk go due to several bizarre and upsetting incidents. Over the last few years, we've used the term Opwynbeylary, a combination of our four names, as a joke about taking over the world. I want to make clear: we are not taking over the world.

It's just that Beyoncé might not be completely on board with the fact that we were joking.

And so my point is that Beyoncé might be plotting the violent overthrow of all world governments. I'm not sure, really. But I think it's a good idea to keep an eye on her.

Hillary

January 6, 2012

TO: HRC
FROM: Barack Obama
RE: Just to keep on your radar

I've been staring at this e-mail a lot over the last 24 hours, and I can no longer tell whether Beyoncé is crazy, you are crazy, or I am crazy.

But okay, 24-hour covert surveillance of Beyoncé. Those agents are going to give us some funny looks when we tell them.

B

March 4, 2012

TO: HRC
FROM: Vladimir Putin
Subject: Pan Bryuchnyy Kostyum

Hello Mrs. Hillary Clinton America!

Guess what I have done! I bought pantsuit company! The one that gives you all those handsome, dignified, dare I say almost Soviet garments. But it is not Mr. Pantsuit anymore. Now it is Pan Bryuchnyy Kostyum, which is Russian for Mr. Pantsuit.

This means that I will always be with you, Mrs. Hillary Clinton America. Those pantsuits are like fabric Putins. I am in your closet, I am in your suitcase, I am always nearby.

March 4, 2012

TO: Huma Abedin
FROM: HRC
FWD: Pantsuits

Please burn all my pantsuits immediately. I'm pretty sure the future of U.S.–Russia relations depends on it somehow. I don't think I'm even exaggerating. And please go to JCPenney or something and buy me a bunch of new pantsuits. Doesn't matter the color anymore.

TO: HRC
FROM: HRC
Subject: Note to Self: Next move

What comes after Secretary of State?

Brainstorm:

Run for President in 2016.

Give a bunch of speeches and make a mountain of cash.
Move to remote seaside village and just take it easy.
Become mayor of seaside village.
Aggressively annex neighboring villages.
Use position to become governor of state seaside village is in.
Use that as a springboard to run for President in 2016.

Write a novel!
Set novel in exciting locales all over the world.
Use experiences in State Department as background material.
Travel the world doing research.
Meet with key diplomats and heads of state.
Write important policy papers and articles and nonfiction books on
the side.
Forget novel.
Use high profile in international affairs to become Secretary of
State.
Or President in 2016.

Move to Nepal and devote life to silent meditation.
yada yada yada
Run for President in 2016.

Hmm. Lots of choices.

★   ★   ★

March 21, 2012

TO: HRC
FROM: Beyoncé
Subject: MY POWER GROWS

HI HILLARY,

JUST WANTED TO LET YOU KNOW THAT EVERY DAY MY POWER GROWS. THE ELEMENTAL FORCES OF THE UNIVERSE GATHER WITHIN MY MIND. LEGIONS OF WARRIORS RALLY TO MY SIDE.

I HAVE EMPLOYED A SOOTHSAYER—HE'S ACTUALLY ALREADY ONE OF MY CHOREOGRAPHERS—WHO GIFTS ME WITH THE VISION OF STANDING ATOP THE UNITED NATIONS WITH A FIERY SWORD IN MY HAND AS ALL THE PEOPLES OF THE WORLD BOW DOWN BEFORE ME.

ALSO, I HOPE THAT MY NOW-SINGULAR QUEST FOR GLOBAL DOMINATION DOES NOT PUT A DAMPER ON OUR SUMMER PLANS. I AM THINKING THE BEACH THIS YEAR.

THE OCEANS WILL RUN RED WITH THE BLOOD OF MY ENEMIES.

BEY

March 21, 2012

TO: Barack Obama
FROM: HRC
FWD: MY POWER GROWS

FYI

H

★   ★   ★

TO: HRC
FROM: Prince
Subject: Hello

Mrs. Clinton,

It's me. Prince.

Eye have heard that U want 2 be with me.

Eye want U 2 know that eye love U 2. Wait—eye don't mean eye love the band U2, I mean that eye also love U as well. U2 is a good band though.

Eye have posters of U all over Paisley Park and eye gaze at them 2 get inspired.

But eye think R love could never B.

Eye am destined 2 love U from a distance.

Because eye am a Mitt Romney supporter. Eye just think he really has some commonsense plans 2 get America on the right track.

Eye had a trained swan type this letter 2 U while eye lounged around in a jumpsuit.

Prince

★ ★ ★

April 4, 2012

TO: HRC
FROM: Huma Abedin
Subject: Wha?

Why are there a bunch of Prince box sets in the garbage can at the front desk?

April 4, 2012

TO: Huma Abedin
FROM: HRC
RE: Wha?

I don't want 2 talk about it.

★ ★ ★

April 10, 2012

TO: HRC
FROM: Huma Abedin
Subject: Passing this along . . .

Got a request from the Boy Scouts for your cookie recipe. Some kind of Mother's Day feature they're doing for their magazine.

April 11, 2012

TO: Huma Abedin
FROM: HRC
RE: Passing this along . . .

Cookie recipe? From the Secretary of State of the United States of America? Of all the things they could ask me about, they want to know about my cookie recipe? Let's send 'em this one. See how they like it.

1 cup flour

2 cups patriarchy (smashed, ground up)

1 cup resentment for being an intelligent, powerful woman

2 1/2 tbsp I'm the Secretary of State, trying to navigate a bloody civil war in Syria and establish a relationship with China that preserves trade and pushes for improved human rights, and you're seriously asking me for a damn COOKIE RECIPE

3 fl. oz. having to work twice as hard as men in similar positions because of how many people within the vast right-wing conspiracy want me to fail

1/2 cup chocolate chips

Put in oven.

Take out of oven, throw it all away, and get back to work.

HRC

May 2, 2012

TO: Barack Obama
FROM: HRC
Subject: Beyoncé threat

Mr. President,

It is my understanding that Beyoncé has constructed a military compound in northern Canada and may have even begun training soldiers. Aerial drones have noticed large banners at the compound that read, "GIRLS WHO RUN THE WORLD." It's the name of one of her songs but also clearly an omen.

Given her tremendous popularity and her lucrative concert appearances, it is not difficult for Beyoncé to amass willing volunteers and arm them with expensive state-of-the-art weaponry.

With your permission, I would like to perform a covert action to stop Beyoncé before she becomes even more of a threat to the global community. I know her best. I can shut her down.

HRC

May 2, 2012

TO: HRC
FROM: Barack Obama
RE: Beyoncé threat

You have the all-clear on my end. I love her music, but I love freedom more. I never expected to have to choose.

B

★ ★ ★

TO: Huma Abedin
FROM: HRC
Subject: Egypt

So far, I think our trip to Cairo has gone well. Only gaffe I can think of is when I kept making jokes about Mohamed Morsi (President of Egypt) and the pop singer Morrissey. These were great jokes!

"Please, Please, Please, Mr. President, let the United States help you get what you want: lasting peace and security in the Middle East!"

"I'm so pleased to meet This Charming Man, Mr. Morsi!"

"Mr. President, I must ask about your Girlfriend in a Coma. How IS she?"

Nothing. Crickets. That's good stuff!

Please arrange to have a selection of Smiths records and Morrissey solo albums delivered to Mr. Morsi at once. Then he'll hear it and get the jokes, and he and I can laugh about it for the long amount of time I'm sure he will be in office.

HRC

★ ★ ★

July 17, 2012

TO: HRC
FROM: The airplane peoples
Subject: Frequent flying

Dear Madam Secretary America,

Congratulations on your recent international trip. With your visits to Laos and Mongolia, you have now visited 102 countries around the world, easily beating the previous record of 96 countries, set by Madeleine Albright, who is not as attractive as you. To date, you have traveled 843,839 miles as Secretary of State.

Not only is this a great achievement for diplomacy, it entitles you to certain rewards. At 100 countries and 843,000 miles, you are entitled to a FREE ALL-EXPENSES-PAID TRIP TO MOSCOW. There you will see such sights as where Vladimir Putin lives and Vladimir Putin fighting five badgers at once and then skinning them and wearing their pelts.

Just tell us when you want to be there!

Sincerely,
The Government. The American One. The real American Government.

Not in Moscow.

★ ★ ★

August 15, 2012

TO: The Fun Three
FROM: HRC
Subject: Operation Swift Response

Ladies,

It feels so weird to send this message to just the two of you and not include Beyoncé. But we do what we have to do. I would like to think that if any of us went rogue and set out to take over the world, the others would act to put a stop to it.

By now, you've both been briefed on what we have to do when we drop into Canada and its Beyoncé-controlled territories tomorrow night.

But just to be sure, let's go over it one more time. We parachute in, each of us landing at a different spot along the perimeter. I take up position near the front door of her makeshift home.

H

August 15, 2012

TO: The Fun Three
FROM: Oprah
RE: Operation Swift Response

Then I knock on the door and act like I'm just stopping by to say hello. We retire to the southeast corner of the house, where there are two large comfy chairs. I ask her what it feels like to be at such an exciting time in her career. Big concerts, so many fans, intentions to take over the world and rule it with an iron fist.

She'll open up to me. This is what I do. I'll Oprah her.

O

August 15, 2012

TO: The Fun Three
FROM: Gwyneth
RE: Operation Swift Response

With her guard down, that's when I show up, also as if stopping by in the remote Canadian wilderness. I'll have a gift basket of fresh produce, eye cream made from the tears of vegan dolphins, and dirt and pumpkin smoothies. All of these products, of course, are laced with sedatives. I am assured these are organic sedatives.

Gwyneth

August 15, 2012

TO: The Fun Three
FROM: HRC
RE: Operation Swift Response

By this point, I'll use my martial arts and small explosives training to subdue any security forces on the scene. I'll put her in a bag and load her onto the waiting helicopter. We hop aboard and then it's off to Washington as the world sleeps on, blissfully unaware of the threat we just neutralized.

Okay, team. Let's do this.

H

August 16, 2012

TO: Barack Obama
FROM: HRC
Subject: Operation Swift Response is complete

We are holding a heavily sedated Beyoncé in the State Department bunker as she undergoes some reeducation exercises. Once we have her fully convinced that it is in everyone's best interests that she concentrates on music instead of global domination, we will release her. She will, of course, be followed by undercover agents posing as fans and photographers for the rest of her life.

Hillary

August 16, 2012

TO: HRC
FROM: Barack Obama
RE: Operation Swift Response is complete

Please release her as soon as possible. If the world discovers that Beyoncé is missing, there will be global panic. Granted, this is preferable to Beyoncé ruling the world as a bloodthirsty tyrant, but it is still a suboptimal result.

TO: Barack Obama
FROM: HRC
RE: Operation Swift Response is complete

Beyoncé appears to have recovered from her imperialist tendencies. I guess all we can do now is let her go, follow her closely, and hope that it is a beloved entertainer we are unleashing on the world. And not a monster.

BTW, as the operation name suggests, we couldn't have done this without some critical input from Taylor Swift, who has a surprisingly tactical mind. Still, I should also point out that Taylor repeatedly murmured something about wanting to stop Beyoncé from "taking what was rightfully mine." So maybe keep an eye on that.

H

August 23, 2012

TO: HRC
FROM: Sarah Palin
Subject: Let's get together!

Hey, the election is coming up! I forget: did we decide that we were going to run together as co-Presidents? I think there's still time! Let's fill out an application!

Or we could see a movie sometime. Hello!

Sarah

August 23, 2012

TO: Sarah Palin
FROM: HRC
RE: Let's get together!

Okay, it IS too late to run for President at this point in time. Barack Obama and Mitt Romney are the two candidates. Also, there is no such thing as co-Presidents, that's just not possible under the Constitution. Furthermore, there is no application.

As for a movie, that sounds great, but I am just far too busy right now and for the next many years.

Oh, by the way, I'm changing my e-mail address. In the future, please send all e-mails to Joe.Biden@whitehouse.gov. Be sure to write often!

Hillary

September 14, 2012

TO: Barack Obama
FROM: HRC
Subject: Benghazi attacks

Obviously, the situation is horrifying and tragic. I will have to be very judicious about the words I choose over the next several weeks and months in discussing it. "We vow to bring the guilty parties to justice," "we will search for how these people were able to carry out their evil plan so we prevent incidents like this in the future," etc.

Even so, I remind you that no one must ever find out the truth. The shocking truth that □□□□□□□□□□□□□□□□□□□□□□□□□□ □□□□□□□□□□□□□□□□□□□□□□□□□□□□□□□□□□□□□□ □□□□□□ and that the State Department believed tha□□□□ □□□□□□□□□□□□□□□□□□□□between Barack Obama and Condi Rice on a speedboat outsi□□□□□□□□□□□□□□ □□□□□□□□□□□□□□□□□□□□□□□□□□Area 51 but by that point, Ed Asner was □□□□□□□□□□□□□□□□□□□ □□□□Whitewater AND Lewinsky AND the repeated failure of the Chicago Cubs becau□□□□□□□□□□□□□□□□□□□□ □□□□□□□□□□□□□□□□□□□□□□□□□□□□□□□□□□□□□□□ □□□□□□□three sorcerers.

[Note from WikiLoox: We are so sorry. We spilled Mountain Dew on the computer right when we had this one pulled up. It's gone. We're really super sorry. So sorry.]

TO: Simon & Schuster
FROM: HRC
Subject: Book titles

Hi book person,

I've thought about it and I think you're right. The world might not be ready for my children's books, my romantic thriller set in the Dirksen Senate Office Building, or my science fiction allegory of the Syrian civil war.

So let's go with the book about my time as Secretary of State. Just brainstorming some titles here.

I Prefer This to Being President

Pantsuits & Problems

Say, She'd Make a GREAT President

We Probably Elected the Wrong Democrat

What It Felt Like to Be Right

50 Shades of Grey (because the issues I deal with are very complex!)

THRILLARY!

The World Didn't Explode, Did It? You're Welcome.

LICENSE TO HILL

Working Hard and Ultimately Not Doing Anything All That Memorable

I know that picking a title for a book isn't easy. It really requires hard choices.

HRC

November 4, 2012

TO: HRC
FROM: Mr. Pantsuit
Subject: Hoping you get this message

Mrs. Clinton,

We don't have much time. We have stolen a guard's laptop when he was asleep. We are imprisoned in a remote part of eastern Russia in an old Soviet camp for dissidents. Somehow we got a Wi-Fi signal.

Our investor, who we are pretty sure at this point was Vladimir Putin, was severely disappointed when we lost your business. "How can I be expected to ever make her mine now?!" he cried. Then he painted a picture of you, forlornly waxed his shirtless torso, recited some very bleak-sounding Russian love poetry, and wept. We understood his feelings for you—some sentiments transcend language—but there was certainly an undercurrent of menace.

The next day, we arrived at work and were accosted by burly goons who placed bags over our heads and put us on a ship. Months later, here we are.

Can you come rescue us? Please?

The staff of Mr. Pantsuit

TO: Barack Obama
FROM: HRC
Subject: Congratulations!

Mr. President,

I am so happy about your reelection and wish to congratulate you on all the hard work that went into it. Obviously, we began our time together as rivals, even enemies, but it has been an honor to serve as Secretary of State in your administration.

As we have discussed, I do wish to step down from the position as soon as a suitable replacement can be found. I hope that this can be a priority now that the election is behind us.

I also hope that I can have your support going forward in any future endeavors I may or may not undertake. If you get my meaning.

HRC

November 6, 2012

TO: HRC
FROM: Barack Obama
RE: Congratulations!

Thank you so much!

And you're talking about running for President in '16, right?

November 6, 2012

TO: Barack Obama
FROM: HRC
RE: Congratulations!

WHAT? Me? Well, gosh, I've been way too busy to even think about doing something like that. President. Wow. That's a new one. Huh.

I mean, if I were to do something like that, I would hope that you'd remember how loyally I served you these past four years, never second-guessing you in the press, always looking for consensus over division. I would also hope you'd remember Bill's speech to the Democratic Convention when he gave you a ringing, passionate endorsement. I would also remind you how I neutralized the Beyoncé threat. So in general, I would think about how much you owe me and how four years from now will be my time. Mine, you hear me, mine all mine.

Okay! Good talk! Enjoy the parties!

HRC

November 30, 2012

TO: HRC
FROM: Joe Biden
Subject: Cheese

Hey Hillary,

Today, I ate a whole brick of extra-sharp cheddar cheese. With a knife and fork. Just sat down and went for it. Sliced off a piece like it was meat loaf, ate it, did it again.

I'm feeling discomfort now. I ate way too much cheese.

Anyway, just wanted to tell you about the cheese. Guess I'll go walk around the office some more. Try to work off this cheese.

Joe

November 30, 2012

TO: Joe Biden
FROM: HRC
RE: Cheese

?

★ ★ ★

TO: Huma Abedin
FROM: HRC
Subject: stupid concussion

Well, I feel pretty lousy. First the stomach virus, then I fall and get a mild concussion. I'm not used to being out of the loop and I don't like it. How are things in the office?

TO: HRC
FROM: Huma Abedin
RE: stupid concussion

Pretty much the same. Everything's under control. You've received some get-well gifts:

- Basket of novels from Oprah

- Basket of, I don't know what it is actually, tree roots? Scrubbing pads? Rocks? They're from Gwyneth and I'm unsure what you're supposed to do with them.

- A Post-it note from Beyoncé saying simply "I SHALL HAVE MY REVENGE"

- A deed transferring the city of Severodvinsk (pop. 192,353) over to you

- A weird kind of hospital gown pantsuit

- Cards from Shonda Rhimes and Vince Gilligan

- A signed photo of Prince and Mitt Romney together at Paisley Park

January 10, 2013

TO: John Kerry
FROM: HRC
Subject: Orientation

Senator Kerry,

I am so delighted that it is you who will be taking my place at the State Department. You bring a keen mind and rich experience to the role and I know you will succeed greatly.

A few recommendations I can make just to get you settled in that much more.

The Wi-Fi reception in the secret underground bunker is terrible. Might want to upgrade that, although almost no one else knows the bunker is there. You open it by taking the Condi Rice autobiography off the shelf and typing in a password, which is "PASSWORD." You should probably change the password.

When you talk to Putin, he might cry. There is nothing you can do about that.

Beware of Beyoncé. That's all I'm saying at the moment, but I'm saying it emphatically. BEWARE OF BEYONCÉ.

Set up a secret e-mail like I did. That way no one will ever get ahold of your correspondences. That's what's so great about e-mail, it's completely untraceable. The ultimate in security. Under no circumstances will it be leaked to someone you don't know. Also, keep that e-mail information away from Joe Biden.

I'm sure we'll be meeting a lot in the weeks to come and I really look forward to it.

HRC

THE DELETED E-MAILS OF HILLARY CLINTON

★ ★ ★

February 1, 2013

TO: Huma Abedin
FROM: HRC
Subject: Last day!

Hey,

I'm headed over to the White House to officially hand in my resignation letter. After that, I know we're all meeting at Applebee's for drinks. I realize that for security purposes, it'll be a special Applebee's set up in the bunker, but I still think it will be fun, especially considering that almost no one on the staff knew the bunker was even there.

H

★ ★ ★

TO: HRC
FROM: Bill
Subject: Last day!

Hey! Congrats on your last day as Secretary of State! You did a great job, no matter what the haters say. Haters gonna hate. I read that somewhere.

I know you have a lot of things to wrap up, but maybe in a couple days we could meet up at Sun Valley for some skiing. Guest list so far: Henry Kissinger, Sammy Hagar, Sandra Bullock, the shadowy men who secretly run our nation's banks, Bruce Willis, Sandra Day O'Connor, Buzz Aldrin, Marilyn Manson, Peyton Manning, Judy Blume, and Prince.

You in?

Bill

ACKNOWLEDGMENTS

Thank you to my family for putting up with me. Thanks also to Peter Clowney, Larissa Anderson, Jennifer Gates, Matt Inman, and Nina's Coffee Café in St. Paul. Additional thanks to Dave the dog because his inclusion will make my kids happy.

ABOUT THE AUTHOR

John Moe is a *McSweeney's* contributor and the host of American Public Media's nationally syndicated public radio show *Wits*. He lives in St. Paul, Minnesota.

WikiLoox is a group of ingenious cyber freedom fighters who comb the remote recesses of the deep Web to gain access to secret, secret, ultrasecret governmental documents. You can find them at www.wikiloox.com.